Ordnance Survey
Snowdonia,
Anglesey and the Lleyn Peninsula
Walks

Pathfinder Guide

Compiled by Brian Conduit

D0277963

Key to colour coding

The walks are divided into three broad categories, indicated by the following colours:

Short, easy walks

Walks of moderate length, likely to involve some modest uphill walking

More challenging walks, which may be longer and/or over more rugged terrain, often with some stiff climbs

Acknowledgements

I am grateful to the following for their valuable advice and assistance: Mr A. Jones (National Park Officer) and Miss M. Rees (Information Officer) of the Snowdonia National Park, and Mr J. Alwyn-Jones, Regional Public Affairs Manager of the National Trust.

While every care has been taken to ensure the accuracy of the route directions, the publishers cannot accept responsibility for errors or omissions, or for changes in details given. It has to be emphasised that the countryside is not static: hedges and fences can be removed, field boundaries can alter, footpaths can be rerouted and changes of ownership can result in the closure or diversion of some concessionary paths. Also paths that are easy and pleasant for walking in fine conditions may become slippery, muddy and difficult in wet weather and stepping stones over rivers and streams may become impassable. If readers know of any changes which have taken place, or have noticed any inaccuracies, Jarrold Publishing would be grateful to hear from them.

Ordnance Survey   ISBN 0-319-00243-8
Jarrold Publishing   ISBN 0-7117-0550-X

First published 1991 by Ordnance Survey and Jarrold Publishing
Reprinted 1993

Ordnance Survey   Jarrold Publishing
Romsey Road   Whitefriars
Maybush   Norwich NR3 1TR
Southampton SO9 4DH

Printed in Great Britain by Jarrold Printing, Norwich. 2/93

Previous page: *the impressive bulk of Harlech Castle*

Contents

Introduction to Snowdonia, Anglesey and the Lleyn Peninsula

Soon after passing through the holiday resort of Colwyn Bay while driving westwards along the North Wales coast road the traveller enters Gwynedd, and shortly afterwards arrives at the broad waters of the Conwy estuary, the eastern frontier of Snowdonia. Across the river stands the impressive bulk of Conwy Castle but beyond that is the first glimpse of the mountains, as exciting an introduction to the region as could be wished for.

Gwynedd is both an ancient kingdom and modern county. In the Middle Ages it was the last stronghold of Welsh independence; today it is the foremost bastion of Welsh language and culture. The mountains of Snowdonia comprise most of Gwynedd but the county includes two other regions: the island of Anglesey to the north and the Lleyn Peninsula to the west — both highly distinctive, both very different in topography from the mountain heartland but sharing with it that same essential 'Welshness'.

From whichever direction they are approached the mountains of Snowdonia present a magnificent spectacle — row upon row of jagged ridges and formidable-looking peaks that have an irresistible appeal to both climber and walker. Presiding imperially over this array is Yr Wyddfa, the highest peak in Britain south of the Scottish Highlands. It is known by its more familiar name, allegedly bestowed upon it by Dark Age sailors, who when voyaging from Ireland to Wales saw snow-covered hills on the skyline and christened them the Snowy Hills or 'Snaudune', initially a collective name that later became restricted to the highest peak only.

The Snowdonia mountains can be divided into a number of clearly defined ranges each with their own characteristics. By far the most popular and most frequently climbed are the Carneddau, Glyders and Snowdon itself in the north of the region. The great ridges and sweeping grassy slopes of the Carneddau cover an extensive area between the Conwy Valley and the Nant Ffrancon Pass and in the north descend abruptly to the coast. Between the Nant Ffrancon and Llanberis passes rise the majestic Glyders, their shattered volcanic rocks creating daunting challenges to the climber and hill-walker and providing the spectacular pinnacles and formations that litter the summits of Glyder Fawr and Glyder Fach. Beyond the Llanberis Pass is Snowdon, its summit accessible by an easy train ride as well as a harder but infinitely more satisfying walk, and to the west of Snowdon the Hebog range forms the western face of the mountains before falling away to the lower hills of Lleyn.

The central zone of Snowdonia comprises the shapely mass of Moel Siabod between the Llugwy and Lledr valleys, the Moelwyns and Cnicht, the latter nicknamed the 'Welsh Matterhorn' because of its instantly recognisable pointed appearance when seen from the west. Also in the central area are the isolated twin Arenig peaks, whose outlines can be seen across the featureless and soggy expanses of the Migneint, looking towards Bala Lake.

On the other side of Bala Lake the Aran range comprises a long ridge running south-westwards towards the Rhinogs and Cadair Idris, which lie close to the Cardigan Bay

Llanddwyn Beach backed by the glorious profile of the mainland mountains

coast. The Rhinogs stretch in a long line from the Vale of Ffestiniog in the north to the Mawddach estuary in the south. Their bare and hard Cambrian rocks, part of a massive upthrust known by geologists as the Harlech Dome, provide some of the roughest and loneliest, but also most rewarding, walking in the whole of the region. To the south of the Mawddach towers the familiar profile of Cadair Idris, not the highest mountain in southern Snowdonia but undoubtedly the best-loved and most popular in Wales south of the Carneddau – Glyders – Snowdon group.

There is more to Snowdonia, however, than mountains. The region has plenty of easy, low-level walks as well as the familiar ascents. Separating the ranges are delightful valleys: some, like the gorges of the Llugwy and Lledr near Betws-y-Coed or the almost perpendicular Aberglaslyn Pass south of Beddgelert, are narrow and steep-sided; others, such as the Dysynni valley below Cadair Idris and the well-wooded Vale of Ffestiniog, are more green and open. Some of these valleys contain remnants of the extensive oak woods that once clothed much of the lower hillsides. Scattered throughout the area are a large number of lakes of varying sizes set amidst varying types of terrain: small lakes like Llyn Idwal and Llyn Cau hemmed in by steep and rocky slopes; larger mountain lakes like the exceptionally beautiful Llyn Gwynant, Llyn Cwm Bychan and Tal-y-llyn; and Bala Lake (Llyn Tegid), the largest natural lake in Wales, situated in more gentle country.

Less dramatic and rugged but equally attractive and absorbing are the landscapes of Anglesey and Lleyn, which not only provide a scenic contrast to Snowdonia but also a wet-weather alternative; often when it is raining in the mountains it may be dry and sunny in these coastal areas.

The long arm of the Lleyn Peninsula has two main attractions for walkers: a line of hills dominated by the three-pronged Yr Eifl along the spine of the peninsula, and a beautiful, varied coastline which couples fine cliff scenery and extensive views with a uniquely appealing sense of remoteness, perhaps not surprising in the vicinity of Braich y Pwll, the 'Land's End of North Wales'. In contrast the island of Anglesey has the flattest terrain in Gwynedd. Here it is the coast that commands the most interest and attention, with paths that wind their way across headlands, through woodlands and along field and cliff edges above some of the finest and most unspoilt sandy beaches in the country.

But from almost any point in Anglesey or Lleyn it is still the Snowdonia mountains that dominate the skyline, whether it be the bold

The Sychnant Pass

ridges of the Carneddau and Snowdon seen from across the Menai Strait, or the impressive profile of the Rhinogs looking across Tremadog Bay from the south coast of Lleyn.

When travelling through Snowdonia, Anglesey and Lleyn the foremost historic remains that catch the eye are the great medieval castles. There are some impressive prehistoric monuments, mainly around the edge of the highland massif in the Conwy Valley, in Anglesey, Lleyn and along the coastal strip. But Roman remains are scanty and the relative poverty of the area means that it is not rich in either ecclesiastical buildings – medieval churches are invariably small and plain though there are some gems – or in large country houses.

The castles, however, are among the finest in Europe. Secure within the natural defences of their mountain fortress and with guaranteed food supplies from Anglesey, the princes of Gwynedd became the most powerful of the native Welsh rulers and in the early thirteenth century Llywelyn the Great probably came nearer to creating a united and independent Welsh nation than any. Imitating the English kings and barons, these princes erected some strong and impressive castles in the late twelfth and early thirteenth centuries and there are substantial remains of these at Dolbadarn, Dolwyddelan (reputed birthplace of Llywelyn the Great), Criccieth (later rebuilt by the English) and the highly atmospheric Castell y Bere.

Llywelyn the Great's death in 1240 was followed by civil wars and in 1272 the accession to the English throne of Edward I, a man determined to extend his authority over all parts of Britain, spelt the end of Welsh independence. Gwynedd was invaded, Llywelyn ap Gruffydd (last native prince of Wales) and his brother were killed and Welsh resistance was crushed. In order to consolidate his conquest Edward I encircled Snowdonia with the formidable and highly expensive castles of Conwy, Beaumaris, Caernarfon and Harlech, all embodying the latest sophistications of castle construction and all built near the coast to allow for easy transport of supplies and reinforcements in case of rebellion. But there were few rebellions, apart from Owain Glyndwr's last brave attempt to forge an independent Wales in the early fifteenth century, and these castles remain as examples of medieval military architecture at its most advanced and refined.

The most striking and large-scale manmade intrusions on the landscape of Snowdonia come from nineteenth- and twentieth-century industrial and commercial developments. Victorian urban expansion created a huge demand for roofing slates, most of which were supplied by the slate quarries of Snowdonia, especially those around Blaenau Ffestiniog, Llanberis and Bethesda. Great scars appeared on the mountain-sides, new settlements rapidly expanded to house the workers, and railways were built to transport the slate from the mines down to the ports at Port Dinorwic, Porthmadog and Twywn. The industry reached its peak at the end of the nineteenth century and subsequently suffered a rapid decline; now only a handful of quarries survive. But although no-one can pretend that these quarries with their waste tips and attendant buildings enhance the landscape, or that the Victorian quarrying villages are picturesque, the remains of this derelict industry and the railways that once served it have become major tourist attractions, an enterprising example of how to turn a scenic eyesore into an asset.

It was around the time that slate-quarrying was starting to develop that the first tourists were beginning to 'discover' Snowdonia. These were the Romantics — artists, writers and intellectuals who were thrilled by the savage and untamed beauty of the region Betws-y-Coed was a particularly popular area for them because of its picturesque location at the meeting of three valleys, its steep wooded hillsides, the proximity of the Swallow Falls and the thickly wooded ravine of the Conwy on which they bestowed the suitably romantic name of the Fairy Glen.

Later the railways brought far greater numbers of visitors into the region — holiday makers to the coastal resorts of Llandudno Barmouth and Aberdovey, and walkers and climbers into the mountains. Of all the recreational opportunities available in Snowdonia, walking and rock-climbing have always been paramount and many Alpine enthusiasts and Himalayan adventurers first 'cut their teeth' on Crib Goch, Tryfan o Cadair Idris.

Tourism has continued to expand to become a vital part of the region's economy but other twentieth-century commercial pressures have had a more significant impact on the landscape: the extensive conifer plantations of Gwydyr, Beddgelert, Coed y Brenin and Dyfi forests, the construction of reservoirs, especially in the valleys of the eastern Carneddau, and the building of the nuclear power station at Trawsfynydd.

In 1951 Snowdonia became a National Park, the second largest of the ten National Parks of England and Wales, and subsequently parts of Anglesey and the Lleyn Peninsula were designated Areas of Outstanding Natural Beauty. Within these three

The wild and remote country of the Rhinogs

areas there are opportunities for walks to suit every conceivable taste, age range and degree of fitness — challenging and strenuous mountain hikes, gentle strolls by rivers and lakes, pleasant woodland rambles and invigorating coastal walks. But wherever you roam the eye is inevitably drawn to those noble mountain ranges that fill the horizon — the Snowy Hills or 'Snaudune' of the early seafarers.

Glossary of Welsh words

aber	estuary, confluence
afon	river
bach, fach	small
bont, pont	bridge
bryn	mound, hill
bwlch	pass
caer	fort
capel	chapel
carn, carnedd	cairn
castell	castle
ceunant	gorge, ravine
coed	wood
craig	crag
crib	narrow ridge
cwm	valley
drws	door, gap (pass)
dyffryn	valley
eglwys, llan	church
fach, bach	small
fawr, mawr	big
ffordd	road
foel, moel	rounded hill
glyn	glen
hen	old
llan, eglwys	church
llyn	lake
maen	stone
mawr, fawr	big
moel, foel	rounded hill
morfa	sea marsh
mynydd	mountain
nant	brook
newydd	new
pair	cauldron
pen	head, top
pont, bont	bridge
pwll	pool
rhaedr	waterfall
sarn	causeway
traeth	beach, shore
twll	hole
ynys	island

The National Parks and countryside recreation

Ten National Parks were created in England and Wales as a result of an Act of Parliament in 1949, and an eleventh was established under special legislation in 1989. In addition to these, there are numerous specially designated Areas of Outstanding Natural Beauty, Country and Regional Parks, Sites of Special Scientific Interest and picnic areas scattered throughout England, Wales and Scotland, all of which share the twin aims of preservation of the countryside and public accessibility and enjoyment.

In trying to define a National Park, one point to bear in mind is that unlike many overseas ones, Britain's National Parks are not owned by the nation. The vast bulk of the land in them is under private ownership. John Dower, whose report in 1945 created their framework, defined a National Park as 'an extensive area of beautiful and relatively wild country in which, for the nation's benefit and by appropriate national decision and action, (a) the characteristic landscape beauty is strictly preserved, (b) access and facilities for public open-air enjoyment are amply provided, (c) wildlife and buildings and places of architectural and historic interest are suitably protected, while (d) established farming use is effectively maintained'.

The concept of having designated areas of protected countryside grew out of a number of factors that appeared towards the end of the nineteenth century; principally greater facilities and opportunities for travel, the development of various conservationist bodies and the establishment of National Parks abroad. Apart from a few of the early individual travellers such as Celia Fiennes and Daniel Defoe, who were usually more concerned with commenting on agricultural improvements, the appearance of towns and

Llyn Cynwch from the Precipice Walk

Cnicht — the 'Welsh Matterhorn'

the extent of antiquities to be found than with the wonders of nature, interest in the countryside as a source of beauty, spiritual refreshment and recreation, and, along with that, an interest in conserving it, did not arise until the Victorian era. Towards the end of the eighteenth century, improvements in road transport enabled the wealthy to visit regions that had hitherto been largely inaccessible and, by the middle of the nineteenth century, the construction of the railways opened up such possibilities to the middle classes and, later on, to the working classes in even greater numbers. At the same time, the Romantic movement was in full swing and, encouraged by the works of Wordsworth, Coleridge and Shelley, interest and enthusiasm for wild places, including the mountain, moorland and hill regions of northern and western Britain, were now in vogue. Eighteenth-century taste had thought of the Scottish Highlands, the Lake District and Snowdonia as places to avoid, preferring controlled order and symmetry in nature as well as in architecture and town planning. But upper and middle class Victorian travellers were thrilled and awed by what they saw as the untamed savagery and wilderness of mountain peaks, deep and secluded gorges, thundering waterfalls, towering cliffs and rocky crags. In addition, there was a growing reaction against the materialism and squalor of Victorian industrialisation and urbanisation and a desire to escape from the formality and artificiality of town life into areas of unspoilt natural beauty.

A result of this was the formation of a number of different societies, all concerned with the 'great outdoors': naturalist groups, rambling clubs and conservationist organisations. One of the earliest of these was the Commons, Open Spaces and Footpaths Preservation Society, originally founded in 1865 to preserve commons and develop public access to the countryside. Particularly influential was the National Trust, set up in 1895 to protect and maintain both places of natural beauty and places of historic interest, and, later on, the Councils for the Preservation of Rural England, Wales and Scotland, three separate bodies that came into being between 1926 and 1928.

The world's first National Park was the Yellowstone Park in the United States, designated in 1872. This was followed by others in Canada, South Africa, Germany, Switzerland, New Zealand and elsewhere, but in Britain such places did not come about until after the Second World War. Proposals for the creation of areas of protected countryside were made before the First World War and during the 1920s and 1930s, but nothing was done. The growing demand from people in towns for access to open country and the reluctance of landowners – particularly those who owned large expanses of uncultivated moorland – to grant it led to a number of ugly incidents, in particular the mass trespass in the Peak District in 1932 when fighting took place between ramblers and gamekeepers and some of the trespassers received stiff prison sentences.

It was in the climate exemplified by the Beveridge Report and the subsequent creation of the welfare state, however, that calls for countryside conservation and access came to fruition in parliament. Based on the recommendations of the Dower Report (1945) and the Hobhouse Committee (1947), the National Parks and Countryside Act of 1949 provided for the designation and preservation of areas both of great scenic beauty and of particular wildlife and scientific interest throughout Britain. More specifically, it provided for the creation of National Parks in England and Wales. Scotland was excluded because, with greater areas of open space and a smaller population, there were fewer pressures on the Scottish countryside and therefore there was felt to be less need for the creation of such protected areas.

A National Parks Commission was set up and over the next eight years ten areas were designated as parks; seven in England (Northumberland, Lake District, North York Moors, Yorkshire Dales, Peak District, Exmoor and Dartmoor) and three in Wales (Snowdonia, Brecon Beacons and Pembrokeshire Coast). At the same time the Commission was also given the responsibility for designating other smaller areas of high recreational and scenic qualities (Areas of Outstanding Natural Beauty), plus the power to propose and develop long-distance footpaths, now called National Trails, though it was not until 1965 that the first of these, the Pennine Way, came into existence.

Further changes came with the Countryside Act of 1968 (a similar one for Scotland had been passed in 1967). The National Parks Commission was replaced by the Countryside Commission, which was now to oversee and review virtually all aspects of countryside conservation, access and provision of recreational amenities. The Country Parks, which were smaller areas of countryside often close to urban areas, came into being. A number of long-distance footpaths were created, followed by an even greater number of unofficial long- or middle-distance paths, devised by individuals, ramblers' groups or local authorities. Provision of car parks and visitor centres, waymarking of public rights of way and the production of leaflets giving suggestions for walking routes all increased, a reflection both of increased leisure and of a greater desire for recreational activity, of which walking in particular, now recognised as the most popular leisure pursuit, has had a great explosion of interest.

In 1989 the Norfolk and Suffolk Broads joined the National Park family, special legislation covering the area's navigational interests as well as aspects of conservation and public enjoyment.

The authorities who administer the individual National Parks have the very difficult task of reconciling the interests of the people who live and earn their living within them with those of the visitors. National Parks, and the other designated areas, are not living museums. Developments of various kinds, in housing, transport and rural industries, are needed. There is pressure to exploit the resources of the area, through more intensive farming, or through increased quarrying and forestry, extraction of minerals or the construction of reservoirs.

In the end it all comes down to a question of balance; a balance between conservation and 'sensitive development'. On the one hand there is a responsibility to preserve and enhance the natural beauty of the National Parks and to promote their enjoyment by the public, and on the other, the needs and well-being of the people living and working in them have to be borne in mind.

The National Trust

Anyone who likes visiting places of natural beauty and/or historic interest has cause to be grateful to the National Trust. Without it, many such places would probably have vanished by now, either under an avalanche of concrete and bricks and mortar or through reservoir construction or blanket afforestation.

It was in response to the pressures on the countryside posed by the relentless march of Victorian industrialisation that the Trust was set up in 1895. Its founders, inspired by the common goals of protecting and conserving Britain's national heritage and widening public access to it, were Sir Robert Hunter, Octavia Hill and Canon Rawnsley; a solicitor, a social reformer and a clergyman respectively. The latter was particularly influential. As a canon of Carlisle Cathedral and vicar of Crosthwaite (near Keswick), he was concerned about threats to the Lake District and had already been active in protecting footpaths and promoting public access to open countryside. After the flooding of Thirlmere in 1879 to create a large reservoir, he and his two colleagues became increasingly convinced that the only effective protection was outright ownership of land.

The purpose of the National Trust is to preserve areas of natural beauty and sites of historic interest by acquisition, holding them in trust for the nation and making them available for public access and enjoyment. Some of its properties have been acquired through purchase, but many have been donated. Nowadays it is not only one of the biggest landowners in the country, but also one of the most active conservation charities, protecting well over half a million acres of land, including over 500 miles of coastline and a large number of historic properties (houses, castles and gardens) in England, Wales and Northern Ireland. (There is a separate National Trust for Scotland, which was set up in 1931.)

Furthermore, once a piece of land has come under Trust ownership, it is difficult for its status to be altered. As a result of Parliamentary legislation in 1907, the Trust was given the right to declare its property inalienable, so ensuring that in any dispute it can appeal directly to Parliament.

As it works towards its dual aims of conserving areas of attractive countryside and encouraging greater public access (not easy to reconcile in this age of mass tourism), the Trust provides an excellent service to walkers by creating new concessionary paths and waymarked trails, by maintaining stiles and footbridges and by combating the ever-increasing problem of footpath erosion.

For details of membership, contact the National Trust at the address on page 78.

The Ramblers' Association

No organisation works more actively to protect and extend the rights and interests of walkers in the countryside than the Ramblers' Association. Its aims (summarised here) are clear: to foster a greater knowledge, love and care of the countryside; to assist in the protection and enhancement of public rights of way and areas of natural beauty; to work for greater public access to the countryside and to encourage more people to take up rambling as a healthy, recreational activity.

It was founded in 1935 when, following the setting up of a National Council of Ramblers' Federation in 1931, a number of federations earlier formed in London, Manchester, the Midlands and elsewhere came together to create a more effective pressure group, to deal with such contemporary problems as the disappearance and obstruction of footpaths, the prevention of access to open mountain and moorland and increasing hostility from landowners. This was the era of the mass trespasses, when there were sometimes violent confrontations between ramblers and gamekeepers, especially on the moorlands of the Peak District.

Since then the Ramblers' Association has played an influential role in preserving and developing the national footpath network, supporting the creation of National Parks and encouraging the designation and way-marking of long-distance footpaths.

Our freedom to walk in the countryside is precarious, and requires constant vigilance. As well as the perennial problems of foot-paths being illegally obstructed, disappearing through lack of use or extinguished by housing or road construction, new dangers can spring up at any time.

It is to meet such problems and dangers that the Ramblers' Association exists and represents the interests of all walkers. The address to write to for information on the Ramblers' Association and how to become a member is given on page 78.

Walkers and the law

The average walker in a National Park or other popular walking area, armed with the appropriate Ordnance Survey map, rein-forced perhaps by a guidebook giving detailed walking instructions, is unlikely to run into legal difficulties, but it is useful to know something about the law relating to public rights of way. The right to walk over certain parts of the countryside has developed over a long period of time, and how such rights came into being and how far they are protected by the law is a complex subject, fascinating in its own right, but too lengthy to be discussed here. The following comments are intended simply to be a helpful guide, backed up by the Countryside Access Charter, a concise summary of walkers' rights and obligations drawn up by the Countryside Commission.

Basically there are two main kinds of public rights of way: footpaths (for walkers only) and bridleways (for walkers, riders on horseback and pedal cyclists). Footpaths and bridleways are shown by broken green lines on Ordnance Survey Pathfinder and Outdoor Leisure maps and broken red lines on Landranger maps. There is also a third category, called byways or 'roads used as a public path': chiefly broad, walled tracks (green lanes) or farm roads, which walkers, riders and cyclists have to share, usually only occasionally, with motor vehicles. Many of these public paths have been in existence for hundreds of years and some even originated as prehistoric trackways and have been in constant use for well over 2,000 years.

The term 'right of way' means exactly what it says. It gives right of passage over what, in the vast majority of cases, is private land, and you are required to keep to the line of the path and not stray onto the land either side. If you inadvertently wander off the right of way — either because of faulty map-reading or because the route is not clearly indicated on the ground — you are technically trespassing and the wisest course is to ask the nearest available person (farmer or fellow walker) to direct you back to the correct route. There are stories of unpleasant confrontations between walkers and farmers at times, but in general most farmers are helpful and co-operative when responding to a genuine and polite request for assistance in route finding.

Obstructions can sometimes be a problem and probably the commonest of these is where a path across a field has been ploughed up. It is legal for a farmer to plough up a path provided that he restores it within two weeks, barring exceptionally bad weather. This does not always happen and here the walker is presented with a dilemma. Does he follow the line of the path, even if this inevitably means treading on crops, or does he use his common sense and walk around the edge of the field? The latter course of action often seems the best but, as this means that you would be trespassing, you are, in law, supposed to keep to the exact line of the path, avoiding unnecessary damage to crops. In the case of other obstructions which may block a path (illegal fences and locked gates etc.), common sense again has to be used in order to negotiate them by the easiest method (detour or removal). If you have any problems negotiating rights of way, you should report the matter to the Rights of Way Department of the relevant county, borough or metropolitan district council. They will then take action with the landowner concerned.

Apart from rights of way enshrined by law, there are a number of other paths available to walkers. Permissive or concessionary paths have been created where a landowner has given permission for the public to use a particular route across his land. The main problem with these is that, as they have been granted as a concession, there is no legal right to use them and therefore they can be extinguished at any time. In practice, many of these concessionary routes have been established on land owned either by large public bodies such as the Forestry Commission, or by a private one, such as the National Trust, and as these mainly encourage walkers to use their paths, they are unlikely to be closed unless a change of ownership occurs.

Walkers also have free access to Country Parks (except where requested to keep away from certain areas for ecological reasons, e.g. wildlife protection, woodland regeneration, safeguarding of rare plants etc.), canal towpaths and most beaches. By custom, though not by right, you are generally free to walk across the open and uncultivated higher land of mountain, moorland and fell, but this varies from area to area and from one season to another — grouse moors, for example, will be out of bounds during the breeding and shooting seasons and some open areas are used as Ministry of Defence firing ranges, for which reason access will be restricted. In some areas the situation has been clarified as a result of 'access agreements' between the landowners and either the county council or the National Park authority, which clearly define when and where you can walk over such open country.

Countryside Access Charter

Your rights of way are:
- Public footpaths — on foot only. Sometimes waymarked in yellow
- Bridleways — on foot, horseback and pedal cycle. Sometimes waymarked in blue
- Byways (usually old roads), most 'roads used as public paths' and, of course, public roads — all traffic has the right of way

Use maps, signs and waymarks to check rights of way. Ordnance Survey Pathfinder and Landranger maps show most public rights of way

On rights of way you can:
- take a pram, pushchair or wheelchair if practicable
- take a dog (on a lead or under close control)
- take a short route round an illegal obstruction or remove it sufficiently to get past

You have a right to go for recreation to:
- public parks and open spaces — on foot
- most commons near older towns and cities — on foot and sometimes on horseback
- private land where the owner has a formal agreement with the local authority

In addition you can use the following by local or established custom or consent, but ask for advice if you are unsure:
- many areas of open country, such as moorland, fell and coastal areas, especially those in the care of the National Trust, and some commons
- some woods and forests, especially those owned by the Forestry Commission
- Country Parks and picnic sites
- most beaches
- canal towpaths
- some private paths and tracks

Consent sometimes extends to horse-riding and cycling

For your information:
- county councils and London boroughs maintain and record rights of way, and register commons
- obstructions, dangerous animals, harassment and misleading signs on rights of way are illegal and you should report them to the county council
- paths across fields can be ploughed, but must normally be reinstated within two weeks
- landowners can require you to leave land to which you have no right of access
- motor vehicles are normally permitted only on roads, byways and some 'roads used as public paths'

The Miners' Bridge spans the gushing waters of the Llugwy above Betws-y-Coed

Key Map 1

Key Map heights shown in feet

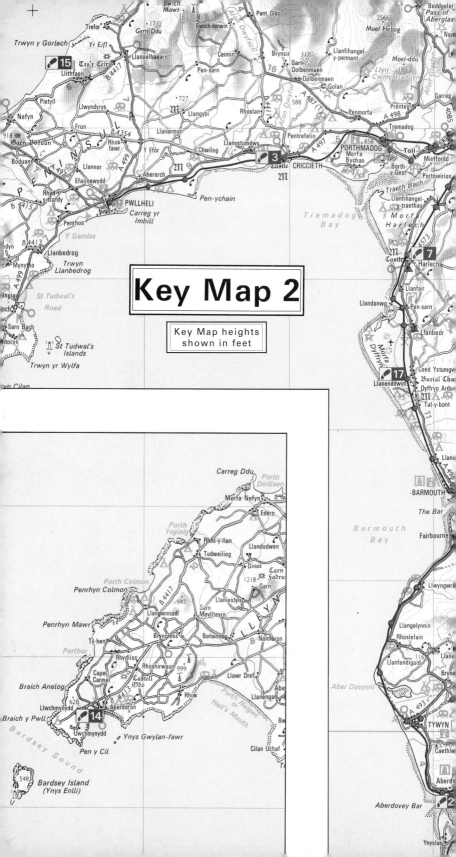

Key Map 2

Key Map heights
shown in feet

CONVENTIONAL SIGNS 1 : 25 000 or 2½ INCHES to 1 MILE

ROADS AND PATHS
Not necessarily rights of way

M1 or A6(M)	M1 or A6(M)	
A 31 (T)	A 31 (T)	Motorway
B 3074	B 3074	Trunk or Main road
A 35	A 35	Secondary road
		Dual carriageway
		Road generally more than 4m wide
		Road generally less than 4m wide
		Other road, drive or track

Unfenced roads and tracks are shown by pecked lines
.... Path

RAILWAYS

	Multiple track	Standard
	Single track	gauge
	Narrow gauge	
	Siding	
	Cutting	
	Embankment	
	Tunnel	
	Road over; road under;	
	Level crossing; station	

PUBLIC RIGHTS OF WAY   Public rights of way may not be evident on the ground

```
------------ }                    + + + + +   Byway open to all traffic
------------ } Public paths {Footpath    
                            {Bridleway    ---   Road used as a public path
```

DANGER AREA
Firing and test ranges in the a
Danger!
Observe warning notices

The indication of a towpath in this book does not necessarily imply a public right of way
The representation of any other road, track or path is no evidence of the existence of a right of way

BOUNDARIES

— . — . — . —	County (England and Wales)
— — — —	District
-o- -o- -o- -o-	London Borough
....	Civil Parish (England)* Community (Wales)
— — — — — —	Constituency (County, Borough, Burgh or European Assembly)

Coincident boundaries are shown b
the first appropriate symbol

*For Ordnance Survey purposes
CountyBoundary is deemed to b
the limit of the parish structure
whether or not a parish area
adjoins

SYMBOLS

▮ Place	with tower	Gravel pit	Water
▲ of	with spire, minaret or dome	Other pit or quarry	Mud
+ worship	without such additions	Sand pit	Sand; sand & shingle
▫ ▢	Building; important building	Refuse or slag heap	National Park or Forest Park Boundary
▨ ▲	Glasshouse; youth hostel	Loose rock	NT National Trust always open
⬭	Bus or coach station	Outcrop	NT National Trust limited access, observe local signs
⛫ ⛫	Lighthouse; beacon	Cliff	FC Forestry Commission
△ ▲	Triangulation pillar	Boulders	
. T; A; R	Telephone: public; AA; RAC	Scree	
▨▨▨▨	Sloping masonry		
---□---- pylon pole	Electricity transmission line		
◦ W, Spr	Well, Spring		
⌖	Site of antiquity		
⚔ 1066	Site of battle (with date)		

VEGETATION   Limits of vegetation are defined by positioning of the symbols but may be delineated also by pecks or dots

Coniferous trees
Non-coniferous trees
Coppice

Orchard
Scrub
Marsh, reeds, saltings.

Bracken, rough grassland
In some areas bracken (⌁) and rough grassland (·······) are shown separately
Heath

Shown collectively as rough grassland on some sheets

In some areas reeds (⌁) and saltings (⌁) are shown separately

HEIGHTS AND ROCK FEATURES

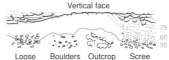

Vertical face

50 · ⎤ Determined ⎡ ground survey
285 · ⎦ by ⎣ air survey

Surface heights are to the nearest metre above mean sea level. Heights shown close to a triangulation pillar refer to the ground level height at the pillar and not necessarily at the summit

Loose rock   Boulders   Outcrop   Scree

75
60   Contours are at
50   5 metres
      vertical interval

TOURIST INFORMATION

✟	Abbey, Cathedral, Priory	❀	Garden	☆	Other tourist feature
🐟	Aquarium	▶	Golf course or links	✕	Picnic site
⋀	Camp site	⊞	Historic house	🚂	Preserved railway
🚐	Caravan site	𝒊	Information centre	🐎	Racecourse
🏰	Castle	⊢⊙⊣	Motor racing	⛷	Skiing
🕳	Cave	🖼	Museum	☀	Viewpoint
Ⴤ	Country park	!	Nature or forest trail	⊥	Wildlife park
⚲	Craft centre	🦆	Nature reserve	🐂	Zoo

P   Parking

𝕮𝖗𝖔𝖘𝖘
SAILING   Selected places of interest

PC   Public Convenience (in rural areas)

𝐶 T   Public Telephone

𝔐 Ancient Monuments and Historic Buildings in the care of the Secretary of State for the Environment which are open to the public

⊕   Mountain rescue post

◄—— ——► National trail or Recreational Path Long Distance Route (Scotland only)

NATIONAL PARK ACCESS LAND
——————— Boundary of National Park access land Private land for which the National Park Planning Board have negotiated public access

Pennine Way   Named path

◄   Access Point

WALKS

[✐1]   Start point of walk   Featured walk   ➡ Route of walk   ▪▪▶▪   Alternative route

ABBREVIATIONS   1 : 25 000 or 2½ INCHES to 1 MILE also 1 : 10 000/1 : 10 560 or 6 INCHES to 1 MILE

BP,BS	Boundary Post or Stone	Mon	Monument	Spr	Spring
CH	Club House	P	Post Office	T	Telephone, public
FV	Ferry Foot or Vehicle	Pol Sta	Police station	A,R	Telephone, AA or RAC
FB	Foot Bridge	PC	Public Convenience	TH	Town Hall
HO	House	PH	Public House	Twr	Tower
MP,MS	Mile Post or stone	Sch	School	W	Well
				Wd Pp	Wind Pump

Abbreviations applicable only to 1 : 10 000/1 : 10 560 or 6 INCHES to 1 MILE

Ch	Church	P	Pole or Post	TCB	Telephone Call Box
F Sta	Fire Station	PW	Place of Worship	TCP	Telephone Call Post
Fn	Fountain	S	Stone	Y	Youth Hostel
GP	Guide Post				

FOLLOW THE COUNTRY CODE
Enjoy the countryside and respect its life and work

Guard against all risk of fire

Fasten all gates

Keep your dogs under close control

Keep to public paths across farmland

Leave livestock, crops and machinery alone

Use gates and stiles to cross fences, hedges and walls

Take your litter home

Help to keep all water clean

Protect wildlife, plants and trees

Take special care on country roads

Make no unnecessary noise

Reproduced by permission of the Countryside Commission

1 Llangower and Bala Lake

Start:	Llangower
Distance:	2½ miles (4 km)
Approximate time:	1 hour
Parking:	Car park and picnic area at Llangower Station
Refreshments:	None
Ordnance Survey maps:	Landranger 125 (Bala & Lake Vyrnwy) and Outdoor Leisure 18 (Snowdonia — Harlech and Bala areas)

Looking across Bala Lake to the Arenigs

General description *Llyn Tegid or Bala Lake lies between the Arenigs and the Arans and is the largest natural lake in Wales, 4 miles (6·5 km) long and ¾ mile (1·25 km) wide. For most of this short, easy but very scenic walk on its south side, there are magnificent views across the lake to the wooded hills opposite, backed by the impressive outlines of the twin Arenig peaks. This is ideal for a leisurely stroll and at the end there is a pleasant lakeside picnic area just over the railway line.*

Between Easter and October the hamlet of Llangower can be reached by taking the Bala Lake Narrow Gauge Railway from Bala Station, where both steam and diesel engines operate on a route that was once the main line between Barmouth and Ruabon. Start by turning right out of the car park and following the road beside the lake for ½ mile (0·75 km) to a public footpath sign by the entrance to Ffynongower **(A)**. Turn left through a metal gate and walk along a gently ascending track to the farm; here turn sharp left up to a metal

gate a few yards ahead. Go through it and keep ahead across a field — from here, and indeed for much of the rest of the walk, there are the most magnificent views to the left over Bala Lake to the Arenigs on the skyline.

Pass through a hedge gap to the right of a large tree, continue steadily uphill to climb a stile and keep ahead to a lane. Cross over, go through a metal gate opposite and walk along a track which curves gently to the right and passes in front of a cottage, going through three metal gates in quick succession. Continue along the left-hand edge of a field, by a line of trees and wire fence on the left, descending into a shallow but steep-sided valley to a stile. Climb it, cross the stream, head up the opposite bank and continue across the grass — there is no obvious path at this stage — beside a line of tree stumps on the left. After climbing a stile in the wire fence ahead follow a grassy path across a field, bearing slightly left towards a farmhouse.

Pass to the right of the farm buildings, bear slightly right, keeping by a wire fence on the left, go through a metal gate and continue gently downhill along a pleasantly tree-lined path into the valley of the Afon Glyn. You join the river briefly and then turn left over a footbridge, bearing left along a grassy path which soon meets a narrow tarmac lane **(B)**. Bear left along this lane, beneath steep, wooded slopes on the right and with fine views of the tree-lined river to the left and the lake and Arenigs ahead, and follow it downhill to a T-junction **(C)**. Turn left along the road for the short distance back to the starting point, passing on the right Llangower's tiny church, which has two interesting features: it stands in a circular graveyard and possesses a funeral bier which used to be carried by a horse at each end.

SCALE 1:25 000 or 2½ INCHES to 1 MILE

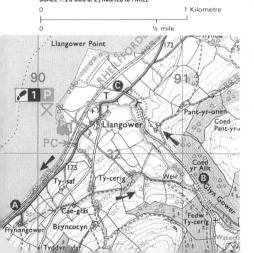

2 Aber Woods and Falls

Start: Bont Newydd, on minor road about ¾ mile (1·25 km) south-east of Aber village

Distance: 3 miles (4·75 km)

Approximate time: 1½ hours

Parking: Roadside parking areas beside Bont Newydd

Refreshments: None

Ordnance Survey maps: Landranger 115 (Snowdon) and Outdoor Leisure 17 (Snowdonia – Snowdon area)

General description *There can be few short walks more pleasant than this – a gentle stroll through a beautifully wooded and steep-sided valley on the northern fringes of Snowdonia to the spectacular Aber Falls. The return leg brings glimpses of the Menai Strait and beyond that Anglesey.*

Start by going through a gate to the right of the bridge, entering Coedydd Aber National Nature Reserve, and take the path ahead through the woods with the river on the left. Soon you turn left over a footbridge, go through a metal gate and turn right **(A)** to keep along a clear, broad track up to the falls, which are in sight for much of the way, a distance of 1¼ miles (2 km). The track climbs gently and proceeds through a delightful mixture of woodland and meadow, with a striking contrast between the deciduous woodland in the valley to the right and the coniferous woodland on the slopes to the left. Nearing the falls climb some steps, pass through a kissing-gate and continue up

The spectacular Aber Falls

SCALE 1:25 000 or 2½ INCHES to 1 MILE

to the foot of Rhaeadr-fawr (the Big Fall), the main and most dramatic fall **(B)**.

Retrace your steps to the kissing-gate; do not go through it but turn right by a wire fence on the left. The fence ends after a few yards; bear slightly left towards another wire fence and head uphill across rough and rocky ground along a narrow but clear, yellow-waymarked path, making for a stile into conifer plantations **(C)**. Climb the stile and ignoring the yellow-waymarked uphill path to the right follow the path ahead through the conifers, heading gently downhill and later keeping along the edge of the plantation to a gate and stile. Climb the stile and continue along the edge of the plantation, by a wire fence on the right – in front the Menai Strait can be seen with Anglesey beyond – still heading gently downhill and bearing gradually left to rejoin the outward route. Turn right to return through the delightful Aber Woods to the starting point.

3 Criccieth and Llanystumdwy

Start:	Criccieth
Distance:	4½ miles (7·25 km)
Approximate time:	2 hours
Parking:	Criccieth
Refreshments:	Pubs, restaurants and cafés at Criccieth, pub and café at Llanystumdwy
Ordnance Survey maps:	Landranger 123 (Lleyn Peninsula) and Pathfinder 822, SH 33/43 (Pwllheli)

General description *This is an easy, half-day stroll in the flat, gentle, wooded coastal area of the Lleyn Peninsula between Criccieth and Llanystumdwy. It is very much 'Lloyd George' country: the great Welsh statesman spent much of his life here and the walk passes the Lloyd George Museum, his grave and memorial above the River Dwyfor, and Ty-newydd, the house in which he spent his last years and where he died. For much of the way there are fine views across Cardigan Bay to the Rhinogs.*

The small, pleasant resort of Criccieth is dominated by its castle, boldly situated on a headland between two fine beaches and looking across Tremadog Bay to Harlech

Criccieth Castle guarding the north side of Tremadog Bay

Castle. It was originally a native Welsh castle, built in the thirteenth century during the reign of Llywelyn the Great, but after Edward I's conquest of Wales it was taken over and extended by the English king to serve as a part of the ring of powerful fortresses encircling Snowdonia. Owain Glyndwr captured and burnt it in 1404 during his uprising and it appears never to have been garrisoned again, falling into disuse and ruin.

The walk starts by the castle entrance. Head downhill in a westerly direction and along the seafront, and where the road bears right in front of a triangular-shaped green keep ahead **(A)** to pass through a kissing-gate, at a footpath sign, onto the coast path. The path keeps along the top of low cliffs, by a wire fence on the right, and makes a slight detour to the right in front of a house, soon turning left over a stile to regain the coast. Soon there are extensive views: ahead down

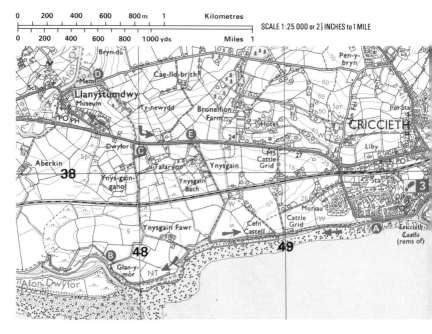

the length of the Lleyn Peninsula, to the right the peaks of Yr Eifl (the Rivals) and to the left the most magnificent views across Cardigan Bay to Harlech Castle and the Rhinogs.

After 1 mile (1·5 km) you reach the estuary of the little River Dwyfor; keep along the riverbank as far as a public footpath sign. Here turn right **(B)** along an enclosed track, climb a stile beside a gate and continue along the track, which bends left then right and finally left again, to reach another stile beside a gate. Climb that, bear left at a T-junction a few yards ahead and keep ahead along a broad, stony track, crossing the railway line and continuing up to the Criccieth – Pwllheli road **(C)**. Turn left along the road and take the first turning on the right through the village of Llanystumdwy, passing the Lloyd George Museum on the right and continuing to the bridge.

Just before the bridge turn right along a lane for a few yards, and at a public footpath sign turn left into the riverside woods to Lloyd George's grave and memorial, designed by the renowned Welsh architect Clough Williams-Ellis, best known for his Italian-style village of Portmeirion, not far away on the opposite side of Tremadog Bay. The oak woods which slope down from here to the River Dwyfor are delightful – especially in spring when carpeted with bluebells – and if time is available it is worth making a diversion to descend to a kissing-gate and take a short stroll through these woods by the river before returning to the memorial and lane.

Continue along the lane and at a public footpath sign turn right **(D)** along the drive to Ty-newydd, bearing left in front of the house where Lloyd George spent his last years and in which he died in 1945. Continue, passing a row of single-storeyed cottages on the left, to a kissing-gate, go through, down some steps and turn right to keep along the edge of fields. Climb some more steps in a wall and turn left downhill along the left-hand edge of a field, by a hedge on the left, to go through a kissing-gate onto the main road again. Turn left along it for ¼ mile (0·5 km) and at a public footpath sign turn right **(E)** down a tree-lined drive. Where the drive bends to the right keep ahead, go up some steps and continue along a path to go up more steps at the side of a house.

Walk along a grassy path, going through a kissing-gate and passing under a very low railway bridge, to continue along what is now a broad, hedge-lined track down to the sea. Turn left on joining the coast path to retrace your steps to Criccieth – a most pleasant finale, with superb views of Criccieth Castle perched on its rock in the foreground and the dramatic skyline of Snowdonia on the horizon.

4 Cwm Pennant

Start:	Gated bridge over River Dwyfor about 1 ½ miles (2·5 km) north of church at Llanfihangel-y-pennant
Distance:	3 ½ miles (5·5 km)
Approximate time:	2 hours
Parking:	Roadside verges just before gated bridge
Refreshments:	None
Ordnance Survey maps:	Landranger 115 (Snowdon) and Outdoor Leisure 17 (Snowdonia – Snowdon area)

General description The wild, remote beauty of Cwm Pennant, the upper reaches of the River Dwyfor, so inspired the Welsh shepherd-poet Eifion Wyn that he is supposed to have said as he lay dying: 'Oh God, why didst Thou make Cwm Pennant so beautiful and the life of an old shepherd so short?' This walk certainly reveals the beauty of the valley, cradled by lonely and impressive mountains on three sides – the Hebog range to the east and Nantille range to the north and west – and linked to the 'outside world' by just one narrow, winding lane. Part of the route follows the track of a disused railway which leads to the remains of quarry buildings, an indication that even this seemingly isolated, untouched and unspoilt area, on the western fringes of Snowdonia, was not immune from Victorian industrial exploitation.

Refer to map overleaf.

The River Dwyfor flows through remote Cwm Pennant

Cross the gated bridge over the River Dwyfor and walk along the lane for ¼ mile (0·5 km) to where it bears left to recross the river (**A**). Here keep ahead along a broad track, go through a metal gate and head gently uphill. Where the track does a U-turn to the right continue straight ahead, by a wall and wire fence on the left, later veering right away from the wall and heading uphill to pass through a metal gate in a wire fence ahead.

On the next section of the walk, until reaching a disused railway track, there is no visible path. Cross a stream and keep ahead roughly in the same direction, skirting to the left of a hill. Just before reaching a short, isolated section of walling turn right and head uphill through bracken, making for the right-hand edge of a small conifer plantation. Keep to the right of the plantation, go through a metal gate and continue in the same direction, heading uphill to meet a flat, grassy track just before a group of boulders (**B**). This is the bed of a disused railway that carried passengers and goods down to Porthmadog until its closure in 1882. Bear left along this track, which provides pleasant, easy walking

with superb views ahead looking up the valley, cross a stream, climb a ladder-stile in front of the buildings of an abandoned slate quarry and clamber up a slope to rejoin the track (**C**).

Here turn left, passing through the ruined buildings, to pick up an easily discernible path, looking out for a ladder-stile on the left. Climb it, continue to a white walker waymark a few yards ahead and then follow a clear grassy path that heads gently downhill between bracken giving superb views, this time looking down the valley. The path is rather indistinct in places but there are regular marker posts. Later you head quite steeply downhill, bearing right at a fork and continuing down towards the river.

Bear left to climb a ladder-stile and then turn right to join a farm track a few yards ahead (**D**). Follow it for 1 mile (1·5 km) — later it becomes a narrow tarmac lane — keeping beside the River Dwyfor, which is sometimes on the right and sometimes on the left, and passing through a succession of gates to return to the starting point just beyond the gated bridge.

5 Precipice Walk

Start:	National Park car park 2½ miles (4 km) north of Dolgellau on road to Llanfachreth
Distance:	3½ miles (5·5 km)
Approximate time:	2 hours
Parking:	National Park car park
Refreshments:	None
Ordnance Survey maps:	Landranger 124 (Dolgellau) and Outdoor Leisure 23 (Snowdonia – Cadair Idris area)

General description This is one of the classic short walks of Snowdonia and is entirely on courtesy paths owned by the Nannau Estate which permits public access. It is most important that the Country Code is observed and in particular that walkers keep to the waymarked paths and close all gates. The route is easy to follow, with plenty of waymarks and a series of information boards; the gradients are modest and the views are magnificent. The views are constantly changing because the route follows an anti-clockwise circuit around the slopes of Foel Cynwch and Foel Faner and every bend reveals new vistas over the Arans, Coed y Brenin Forest, the Mawddach valley and estuary and Cadair Idris. The precipice itself is the western section of the walk, high above the Mawddach, along a path believed to have been made by sheep. The final section is a lovely walk along the shores of Llyn Cynwch.

From the car park turn left for about 100 yards (91 m) along the lane signposted to Hermon and at a Precipice Walk sign (A) turn left along a track which heads gently up through conifers. The track turns right and later turns left in front of a stone cottage from where there is a view to the left of Nannau House, built in 1693 on the site of earlier houses and until the 1960s belonging to the Vaughan family, owners of the estate. It is now a hotel. Climb a ladder-stile, turn right and then turn left to head up to another ladder-stile.

Climb it and continue, by a wall on the right, to a footpath sign straight ahead (B). Follow the wall and direction of the footpath sign uphill to the right, climb a ladder-stile and continue along a narrow path, still by a wall on the right. To the right are grand views over rolling hills to the Arans, with Llanfachreth village and church as prominent landmarks. As the path curves to the left around the hill more superb views open up across the densely wooded slopes of Coed y Brenin Forest. After the next ladder-stile comes the precipice part of the walk – along a narrow but safe path through heather, bilberry, rocks and scree across the western edge of Foel Cynwch, which drops steeply to the Mawddach, giving magnificent distant views of the estuary and Cadair Idris.

Climb another ladder-stile, keep ahead, and as the path approaches the end of the ridge there are especially fine views ahead over Dolgellau, the Mawddach estuary and Cadair Idris. Turn left over a ladder-stile and continue above what are now grassy slopes, the path curving left all the while to reach another ladder-stile. Climb it, keep ahead to Llyn Cynwch, and at a footpath sign turn left (C) to follow a delightful, tree-lined path by the shores of the lake. Go through a metal gate and continue to the end of the lake from where there is possibly the finest view of all, looking across the lake once more to the distinctive and seemingly ubiquitous outline of Cadair Idris. From here keep ahead to rejoin the outward route and retrace your steps to the car park.

SCALE 1:25 000 or 2½ INCHES to 1 MILE

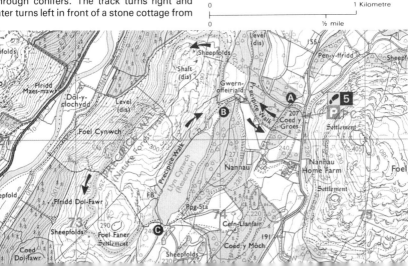

6 Ceunant Cynfal and Ffestiniog

Start:	Bont Newydd, on A470 about 1¼ miles (2 km) south-east of Ffestiniog – turn down lane to south of bridge and bear right at a fork to a stile and footpath sign. Shorter version starts at Ffestiniog
Distance:	4½ miles (7·25 km). Shorter version 3½ miles (5·5 km)
Approximate time:	2½ hours (2 hours for shorter version)
Parking:	Small parking areas beside lane just to west of Bont Newydd near a stile and footpath sign. For shorter version use car park at Ffestiniog
Refreshments:	Pubs at Ffestiniog
Ordnance Survey maps:	Landranger 124 (Dolgellau) and Outdoor Leisure 18 (Snowdonia – Harlech & Bala areas)

General description This walk falls naturally into three parts. The first and last stages go through the delightful woodlands that clothe both sides of Ceunant Cynfal, a beautiful and narrow ravine through which the little River Cynfal cascades over a whole series of falls; in contrast the middle section leads across fields and through more open country to the village of Ffestiniog. This middle part of the route is characterised by the superb views down the thickly wooded Vale of Ffestiniog and across to the imposing 2,527-foot (770 m) bulk of Moelwyn Mawr. The shorter version of the walk, starting at Ffestiniog, joins the main route at point (**B**) below.

At the public footpath sign climb the stile to enter woodland, turn left up some steps and turn right, soon bearing left to follow a narrow, winding, attractive path above the River Cynfal on the right through Ceunant Cynfal – a rocky, tree-lined ravine through which the little river drops over a succession of falls. Pass under the arches of a railway viaduct, climb a stile and cross a footbridge, shortly turning through a gap in the wall on the left and immediately turning right. Continue, between a wire fence on the left and a wall on the right, climb another stile and keep ahead to reach a footbridge below on the right (**A**).

Descend steps to cross it, climb up more steps on the other side and continue along a wooded path to a ladder-stile. Here a short diversion to the left along a path and down steps brings you to the viewing platform for Rhaeadr Cynfal, the most spectacular of the series of waterfalls. Climb the ladder-stile and continue along a pleasant grassy path, by a wall on the right and above a sloping meadow, high up on the right-hand side of the valley. Go through an unusual kissing-gate made of upright slabs of slate and continue gently uphill by a wire fence on the right. Now there are grand views: ahead of Moelwyn Mawr with the wall of the Llyn Stwlan Dam clearly visible, and to the left down the thickly wooded Vale of Ffestiniog. Go through a metal gate, bear slightly left, by a low wall and wire fence on the left, to climb a stile by a footpath sign and head gently downhill, by a wall on the right, passing through another metal gate. Continue downhill between bracken, cross a footbridge over a brook, and by a footpath sign take your choice between climbing a ladder-stile or going through a metal gate. Then head uphill across a field, bearing left and making for a gate. Go through that and turn right to pass through another gate onto a road (**B**). Turn right if visiting Ffestiniog.

Those wishing to do the shorter version of the walk, starting at Ffestiniog, can join the main route at this point, after turning right out of the car park and walking along the road for 100 yards (91 m).

The main route continues by turning left along the road (continuing straight on if coming from Ffestiniog) for just under ¼ mile (0·5 km) to where it bends to the right by a public footpath sign. Here keep ahead through a metal gate and walk along an enclosed track to pass through another metal gate. From here there are fine views down the vale towards the estuary. Head downhill by a wall on the right, pass through a wall gap and continue along a broad grassy track now by a wall on the left, going through another wall gap. After this the path continues between bracken, curving downhill and still by a wall on the left, to the bottom end of the field. Here turn left through a gap in a rather broken-down low wall and continue, by a wall on the right, along a narrow path between bracken to enter woodland, almost immediately climbing a ladder-stile and heading downhill through the trees to a stone stile beside a wall.

Climb it, turn left along the road, cross the bridge over the river and immediately turn left again (**C**), at a public footpath sign, passing

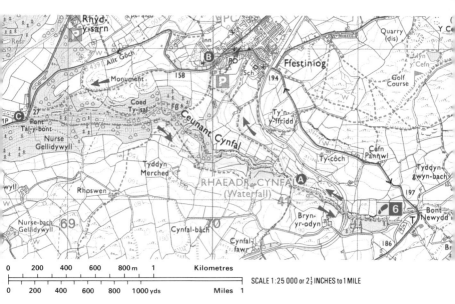

0	200	400	600	800 m	1		Kilometres		
0	200	400	600	800	1000 yds			Miles	1

SCALE 1 : 25 000 or 2½ INCHES to 1 MILE

to the right of a metal gate. Continue along an uphill, wooded track above the River Cynfal on the left, and after passing through a section of rather dark conifers climb a stile to enter attractive broad-leaved woodland again. Soon the path levels off and keeps along the side of the valley to reach an unusually highly decorated wrought-iron gate. Go through it, continue uphill between trees and bracken — Ffestiniog church can be glimpsed to the left on the top of a hill — to go through a metal gate and keep ahead to a stile and public footpath sign.

Climb the stile and continue in the same direction across the next field, bearing slightly left and passing through a gap at the end of it to follow a broad, grassy path between bracken. Bear left again in front of a metal gate and continue, by a wall and wire fence on the right, climbing a stile and re-entering the woodland. Cross a footbridge over a brook, go through a metal gate and keep straight ahead along the edge of more delightful woodland, descending to rejoin the outward route just above a footbridge (A).

For those on the shorter walk, follow the route from (A) to (B) above, then turn right along the road back to the car park in the village.

From here retrace your steps to the starting point — a better direction from which to appreciate the succession of waterfalls on the River Cynfal.

Looking towards Ffestiniog and the Moelwyns

7 Harlech

Start:	Harlech
Distance:	4½ miles (7·25 km). Shorter version 3 miles (4·75 km)
Approximate time:	2½ hours (1½ hours for shorter version)
Parking:	Harlech
Refreshments:	Pubs and cafés at Harlech
Ordnance Survey maps:	Landranger 124 (Dolgellau) and Outdoor Leisure 18 (Snowdonia – Harlech & Bala areas)

General description *It is difficult to envisage a walk that gives finer and more varied views over such a short distance and for such relatively little effort. For almost the whole of this circuit around Harlech there are magnificent and constantly changing vistas over mountains and coast, the majority of them dominated by the imposing bulk of Harlech Castle, one of those rare buildings that blends so well into its surroundings that it appears to be almost an integral part of the natural landscape. The shorter version leads directly back to the town; the full walk includes a bracing stroll over the dunes and along a stretch of the superb, curving, sandy beach that lies below the town and castle walls.*

The small, grey town of Harlech occupies a cliff above the sea; it is huddled around its castle, which is one of the most commanding and spectacularly sited of all the great fortresses built by Edward I to encircle Snowdonia.

The castle had an excellent defensive position: guarding the south side of Tremadog Bay, controlling routeways both along the coast and into the mountains and able to be supplied and reinforced from the sea. When it was built the sea lapped the base of the cliff on which it stands and there was a busy harbour below. Harlech Castle was constructed between 1283 and 1290 and has a basically simple but effective concentric design, with four great rounded towers in each corner and a particularly powerful gatehouse to guard its landward, and therefore most vulnerable, side. Its historic fame revolves around three notable sieges. First it was captured by Owain Glyndwr in 1404 after a long siege – he is alleged to have held an independent Welsh parliament within its walls before its recapture by English forces in 1409. Then it was the last Lancastrian fortress to surrender to the Yorkists in the Wars of the Roses in 1468 – an event which inspired the marching song

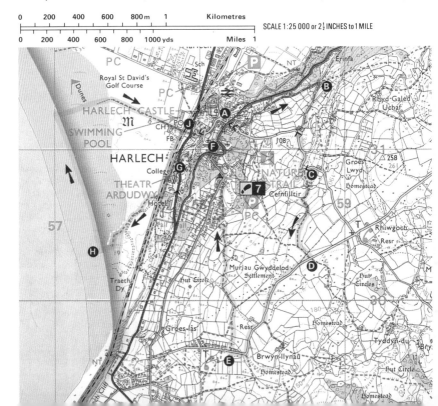

SCALE 1:25 000 or 2½ INCHES to 1 MILE

'Men of Harlech'. Finally in the Civil War of the 1640s it again found fame as the last Royalist stronghold to surrender to Parliamentary forces in 1647.

The walk starts at the car park in the town centre. Turn right and walk along the curving narrow main street, past the small church on the right, to a road junction just above the castle entrance (**A**). Here turn right steeply uphill, passing the Lion Hotel on the right, take the first turning on the left and continue along an uphill lane. From here there is the first of an almost continuous succession of magnificent panoramic views over the castle and town, the dunes of Morfa Harlech, the sweeping curve of the sandy beach, and across the other side of Tremadog Bay to Criccieth Castle, the whole length of the Lleyn Peninsula and the glorious backcloth of Snowdon and the surrounding peaks.

At a T-junction just in front of a cemetery turn left along a track, soon looking out for a public footpath notice; here bear left along an enclosed downhill path above woodland on the left. At the next public footpath sign, at the end of a lane and a turning circle, keep ahead along a path, passing a house on the right, go through a metal gate and continue, by a wall on the right, to another metal gate. Go through that, keep ahead for a few yards to a public footpath sign and here turn sharp right (**B**) along an uphill path, by a wall on the right and rocky outcrops on the left, continuing by the wall and passing through a series of metal gates near farm buildings to come out onto a lane.

Turn left along this narrow, winding, uphill lane, passing in front of a house, and a few yards after a sharp left-hand bend turn right (**C**) through a metal gate and walk along a steadily ascending path, passing between farm buildings and on through two metal gates in quick succession. Continue along a track enclosed by walls and where these end turn left uphill along the left-hand edge of a meadow, by a wall on the left. Go through a wall gap and continue, bearing slightly right, still by a wall on the left, and passing through another gap. Now turn right and head across open country, keeping parallel to a wall on the right, later bearing slightly left away from it to a marker-post. Continue past this to climb a waymarked stone stile, from which there are fine views ahead of the Rhinogs and to the right of Shell Island and the Mawddach estuary. Keep ahead for a short distance to climb a stile by a public footpath sign and turn right along a lane (**D**).

The lane heads downhill — in the field on the right can be seen the remains of the hut circles of Muriau Gwyddelod — and after about 1 mile (1·5 km) you reach a footpath sign (**E**). Here turn right through a small metal gate and walk across a field of rough

grass and bracken, roughly parallel with a wall on the left. At the far end turn left along a grassy track enclosed by walls to head downhill, and after a short distance turn right through a gap in the wall. Immediately turn left to continue downhill along another grassy track, now with the wall on the left, pass through another gap and turn right, following the track to a waymarked stone stile. Climb it and continue in the same direction across the next field — the route is marked by yellow splashes on rocks — to go through a wall gap and keep ahead, passing through another wall gap and heading downhill to a metal gate. Go through that and immediately turn right along an enclosed track, by houses on the left, passing through a metal gate to a footpath sign and from there continuing along a path, between walls and trees both sides, down to a road. Turn right and follow the road as it bends to the left downhill and curves right to a T-junction (**F**).

For the shorter version of the walk turn right here back into Harlech town centre.

Turn left and where the road curves to the left keep ahead at a footpath sign — it is from the rocky outcrop to the right that the traditional picture postcard view of Harlech Castle backed by the Snowdonia peaks is taken. Follow a twisting path down steps and through trees to the main road (**G**), turn right for a few yards and then turn sharp left along a tarmac lane, between the buildings of Coleg Harlech on the left and the railway line on the right. Just after the lane becomes a rough track turn right through a gate to cross the railway line, go through another gate and bear left, clipping the corner of a golf course, to follow a winding track towards the dunes. Where the track bears left keep ahead over the dunes to reach the broad, flat, sandy beach (**H**). Turn right along this splendid beach, from which Criccieth Castle can be clearly seen on its rock guarding the other side of Tremadog Bay, and after about ½ mile (0·75 km) turn right to head back over the dunes. There is no clear indication as to where to leave the beach but keep roughly in line with the castle ahead and on reaching the edge of the golf course look out for and make towards a clear path that can be seen heading in a straight line across the course. This path starts beside a bench; follow it across the course, recrossing the railway line and continuing up to a metal gate and back onto the main road (**J**).

Cross over to a footpath sign, climb a flight of steps to come out on to a road and follow the road steeply uphill around several sharp bends, passing to the right of the castle and continuing up to a crossroads. Turn right along the main street back to the car park.

8 Capel Garmon and the Fairy Glen

Start:	Capel Garmon
Distance:	4 ½ miles (7·25 km)
Approximate time:	2 ½ hours
Parking:	Roadside parking at Capel Garmon
Refreshments:	Pub at Capel Garmon
Ordnance Survey maps:	Landranger 116 (Denbigh & Colwyn Bay) and Outdoor Leisure 16 (Snowdonia – Conwy Valley area)

General description *This walk clearly reveals why the Conwy Valley area so enchanted early Victorian visitors. It starts high up on the eastern side of the valley, from where there are magnificent panoramic views across Snowdonia, and descends gently, via a prehistoric burial chamber, to the river just above the Conwy Falls. Then there is an*

Looking towards the Fairy Glen near Betws-y-Coed

outstandingly beautiful ramble through old oak woodland along the side of the Conwy gorge, with an opportunity to make a brief detour to visit the spectacular Fairy Glen. A stiff climb through more woodland is followed by a gentler climb along a quiet winding lane back to the starting point.

Start by walking through the village, passing the small church on the right and the White Horse Inn on the left, and continue along the road for just under ½ mile (0·75 km); immediately there are superb panoramic views to the right looking across the Conwy Valley to the Carneddau range. At a public footpath sign turn right **(A)** over a ladder-stile and walk downhill along the left-hand edge of a field, by a wire fence on the left, go through a metal gate and continue to another metal gate by farm buildings. Go through that, and another one a few yards in front, and keep ahead to pass to the left of a house. At a sign for 'Burial Chamber' turn right through a metal gate and head across a field, keeping by the right-hand edge, by a wire fence on the right, and turning right through a metal gate at a white arrow waymark halfway along this field. Walk across the next field to the burial chamber, which is ringed by fencing.

A notice says that it was erected in the later Neolithic period, 2500 – 1900 BC, for communal burial, was originally covered by a mound of stones and is similar in design to the long barrows found in south-east Wales and the Cotswolds. It has a fine position with grand views over the mountains.

Just beyond the chamber go through a kissing-gate in the wall in front and continue, looking out for a footpath sign and bearing left in its direction to pass through another kissing-gate. Keep ahead to a group of trees and head across a field to another footpath sign; here turn right along a track which continues downhill to a farm. Follow a footpath sign to the right of the farmhouse, pass through a metal gate and continue between farm buildings to turn right along a tarmac track **(B)**. Keep along the track to another metal gate, go through it and bear left to follow the track as it curves across an open and rocky landscape, with views of the thick woodland that clothes the other side of the valley ahead. The track winds downhill, goes through a metal gate and continues to the A5.

Turn right along the busy main road (be careful – there is no footpath), crossing it to the Conwy Falls Café if you want to pay to visit the Conwy Falls. Otherwise continue along the road and just after it bends to the left **(C)** go down three steps at the end of a small layby and take the path which heads gently downhill through the trees into the Conwy gorge. This path follows the line of

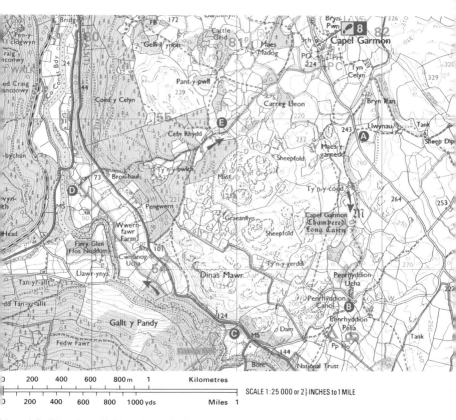

the original London – Holyhead road before Telford built the new road, the present A5, in the early nineteenth century. It is not a legal right of way but the Voelas Estate has traditionally allowed walkers to use it in conjunction with access to the Fairy Glen. It is important that walkers observe the Country Code and the trustees of the estate reserve the right to close the path at any time. (In the event of the latter, continue along the road from **(C)** to where the path crosses it to the east of Point **(D)**.)

Keep above the right-hand side of this beautiful, thickly wooded gorge, a remnant of the extensive oak woods that once clothed much of the Conwy Valley, climbing a series of ladder-stiles. The river can sometimes be glimpsed between the trees on the left and can always be heard as it thunders over the falls far below. After the gorge broadens out there are more fine views looking up the Lledr valley to the left.

After passing through a gate follow the path which descends gently to a stone hut and opposite this there is a gate into the Fairy Glen. Here you can make a brief detour along a path which descends through woods down a series of steps to where the river narrows and squeezes through the rocky, almost perpendicular, tree-lined ravine, so admired

by Victorian visitors who bestowed upon it what they considered a suitably 'romantic' name.

From the gate into the Fairy Glen continue along the now broader track and just after passing through a metal gate, about 100 yards (92 m) before the track bears right, turn right **(D)** towards a house, go through a gate on the right and turn left along the edge of a field, passing to the right of the house. Go through another gate and turn right to keep by a wall on the right, heading uphill and passing through a gate onto the main road again.

Cross over, go through a gap in the wall immediately opposite and bear slightly right along a path which heads steeply uphill, between the edge of woodland on the left and a wall on the right. The path bears slightly left to enter the wood and shortly afterwards turns sharp left to continue steeply up a zigzag path, later keeping along the edge of the wood, by a wall on the right, to join a track. Turn right along the track, climbing gently to emerge from the conifers, with pleasant views of open, hilly country ahead. Go through a metal gate and continue along a narrow lane **(E)** which winds steadily uphill into Capel Garmon, turning left in the village back to the starting point.

29

9 Penmaenpool and the River Mawddach

Start: Penmaenpool

Distance: 5 miles (8 km)

Approximate time: 2½ hours

Parking: Penmaenpool

Refreshments: Hotel at Penmaenpool

Ordnance Survey maps: Landranger 124 (Dolgellau) and Outdoor Leisure 18 (Snowdonia — Harlech & Bala areas)

General description *This is an undemanding walk which for remarkably little effort provides outstanding views, especially of Cadair Idris and the Mawddach estuary. It includes some fine woodland sections and finishes with a relaxing stroll along the south side of the estuary — acclaimed as one of the most beautiful in Europe — using the track of a disused railway.*

Who long for rest, who look for pleasure
Away from counter, court or school
O where live well your lease of leisure
But here, here at Penmaenpool.

So wrote Gerard Manley Hopkins in 1876, but nowadays Penmaenpool is even quieter. Indeed it is hard to believe that this tiny hamlet at the southern end of a wooden toll bridge across the Mawddach was once a shipping and shipbuilding centre. Both the railway that ran along the estuary from Barmouth Junction (now renamed Morfa Mawddach) to Dolgellau and the station at Penmaenpool had lifespans of exactly a century, opened in 1865 and closed in 1965. At least this disused railway now serves useful purposes: the line as a footpath and the former signal-box at Penmaenpool as an RSPB Nature and Wildlife Centre.

From the car park turn right along the road in the Tywyn direction and at a footpath sign turn sharp left **(A)** along a winding, uphill, woodland path. Go through a metal gate, turn left along a track, following yellow waymarks, and bear right at a fork, continuing gently uphill all the time through woodland. Look out for a yellow waymark on the right, opposite a small pool, and turn right along a narrow path which continues more steeply through trees, climbing some steps to reach a ladder-stile.

Climb it to emerge from the trees and in front is a superb view of Cadair Idris. Keep ahead, bearing right along a clear track at a waymark. The track soon bears to the right but you continue ahead towards a house, going through a metal gate, passing in front of the house and on through another metal gate. Now turn right to walk along a narrow field, keeping by a wall on the left, to a ladder-stile beside a gate; turn left over it and continue along a track to another ladder-stile by a gate. Climb it and keep ahead to farm

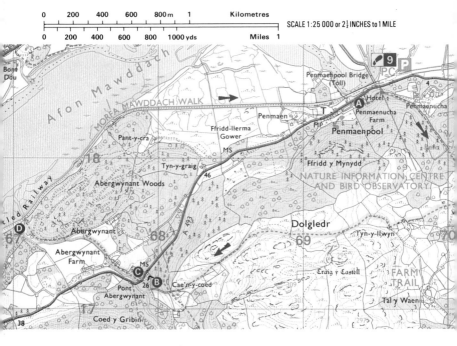

The River Mawddach at idyllic Penmaenpool

uildings; here turn right up to a waymarked metal gate.

Go through and turn left uphill, bearing lightly to the right away from the wall on the eft and making for a marker-post. Here turn ght along a track, cross a small stream, urve left to pass through a wall gap and ontinue gently uphill, by a wire fence and ater a wall on the left. Go through a metal ate, keep ahead to a marker-post, then bear ght to follow a grassy uphill track over the dge – there are superb views from here ver the Mawddach estuary – and continue a stone stile in the wall ahead. This is omewhat difficult to spot. Climb over and urn right along a broad, curving farm track, ollowing it downhill, climbing a ladder-stile eside a gate and finally going through a metal gate onto a road **(B)**. Turn right along he road, heading downhill through voodland, bending sharply left and ontinuing more steeply down to the main Dolgellau – Tywyn road.

Turn left for a few yards and just before a bridge turn right **(C)** along a tarmac track to Abergwynant Farm. This delightful track keeps by the rocky waters of the River Gwynant on the left all the while to where it joins the Mawddach. Go through a metal gate at a bridge and continue, passing through another metal gate to enter woodland. The track curves to the left to continue below the steep slopes of Abergwynant Woods and where it later bears right keep ahead to a marker-post, continue past it to cross a footbridge and bear right to ascend to the disused railway track **(D)**.

Turn right to follow the track for just over 1½ miles (2·5 km) to Penmaenpool – a lovely, relaxing finale with grand views across the Mawddach estuary all the while. Just before the end you pass through a wooded gully, crossing the neck of the headland of Penmaenpool; continue through a kissing-gate to the George III Hotel, bridge and car park.

31

10 Newborough Forest and Llanddwyn Island

Start:	Newborough
Distance:	7 miles (11·25 km). Shorter version 5½ miles (8·75 km)
Approximate time:	3½ hours (2½ hours for shorter version)
Parking:	Newborough
Refreshments:	Pub and café at Newborough
Ordnance Survey maps:	Landrangers 114 (Anglesey) and 115 (Snowdon), Pathfinder 768, SH 36/46/56 (Caernarfon)

General description *Here is a walk that is in total contrast to most in this book – a mainly seashore and forest walk across predominantly flat terrain in the south-west corner of Anglesey, visiting a ruined church and passing the edge of one of the most extensive sand-dune systems in Britain. The superb views across the Menai Strait to Snowdonia and the hills of Lleyn are a constant reminder, however, that the mountains are not far away and still dominate the landscape. The shorter version of the walk omits Llanddwyn Island and its ruined church.*

The walk begins at the crossroads in Newborough, a village so called because in 1295 people from the village of Llanfaes, evicted from their homes by Edward I during the building of Beaumaris Castle, were resettled here in his 'new borough'. Shortly afterwards the early fourteenth-century church was built to the south.

Take the road signposted to Llanddwyn Beach, head slightly uphill out of the village and turn right along a tarmac track by the side of the church **(A)**. Go through a kissing-gate, keep ahead to the end of the church wall and turn left through another gate, still by the church wall on the left. Continuing past the church go through a gate, walk across a field to climb a ladder-stile and keep along the edge of the next field to climb another one. At this point there are fine views: to the left across to Snowdonia, ahead to the dark green, unbroken mass of the forest, and to the right Malltraeth Sands and the Cefni estuary. Continue across the next field in the same direction, later keeping by a wire fence on the right, bear slightly left to pass through a metal kissing-gate and

keep ahead to a ladder-stile. Climb it and continue towards the dark mass of conifers in front along a recognisable path which joins a grassy track coming in from the left.

Climb a stile to the left of a metal gate to enter Newborough Forest **(B)**. This plantation was begun by the Forestry Commission in 1948 and comprises about 2,000 acres, mostly of Corsican pine. For the next 1½ miles (2·5 km) follow a pleasant broad track through the forest to Llanddwyn Beach: at the first fork take the right-hand track, keep ahead at a crossroads of tracks after which the grassy track becomes made-up forest road, and after reaching a circular enclosure bear right along a sand track through the dunes to the beach **(C)**.

*Those wishing to do the shorter version which omits Llanddwyn Island should turn left here along the beach, following the route after **(C)** below.*

Turn right along this superb beach and, tides permitting, bear left to follow a path across the narrow peninsula to the lighthouse **(D)** at the tip of Llanddwyn Island. This is only an island at high tide, but walkers should time their visit so as not to get cut off. Near the lighthouse are the scanty but atmospheric ruins of a sixteenth-century church. Please keep to the path as the island is part of the Newborough Warren Nature Reserve.

Retrace your steps to where you first joined the beach **(C)** and continue along the crescent-shaped, sweeping expanse of sand

SCALE 1:25 000 or 2½ INCHES to 1 MILE

with glorious views across the Menai Strait to Snowdonia and the hills of Lleyn. Keep looking to the left over the high dunes and at the point where the trees end (E) search for a relatively easy place to scramble up the dunes. At the top keep to the left of a wire fence, descending slightly to join a path along the right-hand edge of the forest. Keep along this lovely, undulating path for 1 mile (1·5 km), between the edge of the forest on the left and Newborough Warren on the right, the latter a National Nature Reserve and one of the largest areas of dunes in the country. The views across the dunes to the mountains on the horizon are superb.

On reaching the end of the forest continue along the path and soon the houses of Newborough come into view on the low ridge across the fields to the left. Shortly afterwards at a crossroads of paths (F) turn left along an attractive, broad, green, hedge-lined track, which later becomes a rough tarmac track and later on a lane, heading gently uphill towards Newborough church. Keep ahead on joining the road and follow it round to the right back into the village.

11 The Dysynni valley and Castell y Bere

Start:	Llanfihangel-y-pennant
Distance:	6 miles (9·5 km)
Approximate time:	3 hours
Parking:	Llanfihangel-y-pennant, or car park about ¼ mile (0·5 km) to the east at Castell y Bere
Refreshments:	Café and pub at Abergynolwyn (entails a brief detour)
Ordnance Survey maps:	Landranger 124 (Dolgellau) and Outdoor Leisure 23 (Snowdonia – Cadair Idris area)

General description   *Much of this route is in the quiet, hilly, attractively wooded country of the Dysynni and Cadair valleys, surrounded by mountains and lying near the foot of Cadair Idris. It is a relaxing walk with only a few gentle gradients and has a pleasantly remote feel about it. Historic interest is provided by the medieval church at Llanfihangel-y-pennant, the ruins of Castell y Bere and the remains of Mary Jones' cottage. The most dramatic scenic feature is the view, from a number of different points in the latter stages of the walk, of Craig yr Aderyn or Birds' Rock.*

The tiny, isolated church at Llanfihangel-y-pennant, though much restored in Victorian times, is a delightful old building which dates back to the twelfth century. In the north wall near the door of the vestry is a lepers' window; lepers were not allowed into the church but could watch the service from here. The village that the church served has almost disappeared – now there are only a handful of cottages and farms.

Start by walking away from the church along a signposted path at the side of the car park, passing a house on the right. Climb a ladder-stile, keep ahead to enter woodland, by a stream on the right, and follow yellow waymarks up beside a virtual mini-gorge and a series of falls, climbing between trees and bracken to the top of the falls. Bearing slightly to the left continue steeply uphill, climb a stile and turn right to keep by the stream through a lovely, remote valley which now broadens out. The path is not always clear but continue roughly in a straight line, with the stream below on the right all the time, eventually crossing it just before a ruined farm.

Bear slightly left to climb a ladder-stile and continue through the valley, bearing right by a broken wall on the right and passing through a gap in the wall to a ladder-stile. Climb it and follow the clear track ahead which curves left downhill into woodland, with magnificent views ahead over the Dysynni valley. Look carefully for a yellow post to the right of the track (this could easily be missed); here turn sharp right along a narrow waymarked path which zigzags steeply downhill through the trees to a ladder-stile. Climb it, continue downhill across the field ahead, climb another ladder-stile in the far corner and turn sharp right along a lane signposted to Llanegryn **(A)**.

The lane climbs above the river on the left and you follow it for 1¼ miles (2 km), passing above the former slate-quarrying village of Abergynolwyn, whose appearance even from a distance indicates that it was built on more spacious and advanced lines than most others of its time. For a closer look (and some refreshments) you can make a brief detour to the left down some steps at a public footpath sign **(B)**, turning right along the river into the village and rejoining the main route at **(C)** by turning right by the bridge and following the lane uphill. Otherwise keep ahead to the junction of lanes **(C)** and turn right (continue straight on if coming from Abergynolwyn) along the lane signposted Llanfihangel and Castell y Bere to continue through the increasingly narrow and steep-sided valley of the River Dysynni for just under ½ mile (0·75 km).

Look out for a public footpath sign above you on the right **(D)** and head up to it to climb a stile. Follow a path diagonally over the shoulder of Foel Cae'rberllan, at first keeping roughly parallel with the lane below on the left but later bearing right along a rather indistinct path and heading downhill to join a wall on the right. Cross a stream and continue along the edge of beautiful scattered woodland on the left, following the wall downhill and bearing right to a metal gate. Go through it, keep ahead to pass through a second one, do not go through a third one but bear left to climb a stile beside it. From here there is a superb view of Castell y Bere. Continue downhill along a narrow but discernible path in the direction of the castle to join a track below, bear right along it, turn left through a metal kissing-gate and then turn half-right to head diagonally across a field to a stile and public footpath sign.

Climb the stile and turn sharp left along a lane, below the wooded rocky outcrop crowned by the scanty but nevertheless atmospheric and romantic-looking remains of Castell y Bere. Part of its romance lies in its dramatic situation above the valley with grand views downstream to the distinctive profile of Birds' Rock, and part is because it is a native Welsh castle, unlike most of the other castles of Snowdonia which were built by the English conquerors. It was begun by Llywelyn the Great in the early thirteenth century, captured by English forces in 1283 during Edward I's conquest of Wales and briefly reoccupied by the Welsh in the 1294 rebellion. After that it seems to have been abandoned.

Continue along the lane as far as a footpath sign and turn right over a stile (**E**). Walk along the edge of a field, following the field edge to the right below the castle to cross a footbridge and climb a ladder-stile. Now turn right along the edge of the next field, by a wire fence on the right, turning right through a metal gate at the end of the field and then turning left to follow a tarmac drive through a farmyard. Go through a metal gate and keep ahead to cross a footbridge over the River Cadair. From the bridge there is a superb view to the left of Craig yr Aderyn (Birds' Rock), 762 feet (232 m) high and once lapped by the sea. It is the only place in Britain not on the coast where cormorants nest. Go through another metal gate and turn right (**F**) to follow an attractive, grassy path beside the river — after passing a house on the left it widens into a track — over a series of stiles and finally through a gate onto a lane (**G**).

Looking towards Birds' Rock from the atmospheric ruins of Castell y Bere

Opposite is the ruined cottage of Tyn-y-ddol and monument to Mary Jones who lived here. The story of this sixteen-year-old daughter of a poor weaver who in 1800 walked barefoot and alone over the mountains to Bala, a distance of nearly 30 miles (48 km), to buy a Welsh bible, has become a legend. When she arrived there the last one had been sold but the Methodist minister, Thomas Charles, not only gave her his own bible but was so impressed by her courage and determination that he started the movement that was to lead to the founding of the British and Foreign Bible Society.

Turn right to cross the river and follow the lane for ½ mile (0·75 km) back to Llanfihangel-y-pennant, an attractive finale because of the fine views of the three main features of the walk — the church, beyond that the castle and beyond that Birds' Rock.

SCALE 1:25 000 or 2½ INCHES to 1 MILE

12 Conwy Mountain and the Sychnant Pass

Start:	Conwy
Distance:	6 miles (9·5 km)
Approximate time:	3 hours
Parking:	Conwy
Refreshments:	Pubs, restaurants and cafés at Conwy
Ordnance Survey maps:	Landranger 115 (Snowdon) and Outdoor Leisure 16 (Snowdonia – Conwy Valley area)

General description *It is not surprising that Conwy Mountain is one of the most popular walking areas in northern Snowdonia. Its breezy, gorse- and bracken-covered slopes offer several irresistible advantages: easy accessibility, proximity to one of the most delightful and historic towns in Wales, clear paths, relatively easy climbing (despite its name Conwy Mountain rises only to the modest height of 809 feet (247 m)) and, best of all, the most magnificent panoramic views both inland and over the coast and estuary. There are many possible walks; this one goes over the mountain to the head of the spectacular Sychnant Pass and returns to Conwy via a gentler, lower-level route.*

Conwy is one of the most perfect medieval walled towns in Europe. Splendidly situated overlooking a broad estuary and commanding one of the main routes into the heart of Snowdonia, it is easy to see why it was of such strategic significance in the English conquest of Wales. Here Edward I constructed one of his grandest and most expensive fortresses, built in the remarkably short time of five years (1283 – 7), a gigantic feat of labour and organisation. It is one of the chain of castles that he built encircling Snowdonia, the last bastion of Welsh resistance, to try to fasten English rule on this wild and unruly area. Linked to it is a circuit of walls, still almost complete and a most attractive and interesting walk in themselves. Within the walls are a number of fine old buildings: the fourteenth-century parish church occupying the site of the Cistercian abbey of Aberconwy, moved by Edward I when he built his castle; Aberconwy House, a rare example of a thirteenth-century merchant's house; the impressive sixteenth-century town house of Plas Mawr; and, down on the quayside, a cottage which claims to be the smallest house in Britain.

Inevitably the castle dominates the town but almost as imposing is the series of bridges across the Conwy estuary. The earliest of these is Telford's suspension bridge of 1826, now a historic monument owned by the National Trust, followed by Robert Stephenson's tubular railway bridge built about twenty years later and castellated to harmonise with the castle walls. By the 1950s Telford's bridge was no longer

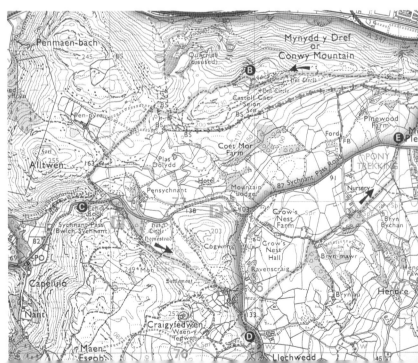

dequate for the volume of traffic and a new oad bridge was built alongside it. In turn this as failed to solve Conwy's notorious traffic roblem and the latest project, currently nder way, is the construction of a tunnel nder the estuary.

The walk starts in front of the castle. Walk long the main road (Rose Hill Street) in the angor direction, pass through a gap in the nedieval walls and keep ahead for a short istance before turning left into Cadnant ark, in the direction signposted Conwy Mountain and Sychnant Pass **(A)**. Cross the ailway, turn right parallel to the railway line, nd shortly after the road curves to the left urn right down Mountain Road. This road oon narrows to little more than a tarmac rack and at a footpath sign bear right gnoring the direction of the sign which is long the broad track straight ahead) to ollow a narrow, winding, uphill path, hrough bracken and gorse, that keeps oughly parallel with the lower track as it eads up the side of the hill. Continue along his steadily ascending path — Conwy Mountain is criss-crossed with paths — earing right at a fork and then bearing left nto the ridge. Follow the ridge to its highest oint **(B)** from where the all-round panoramic iews over the town, estuary, Great Orme, landudno, the Carneddau, the coast, the Menai Strait and the island of Anglesey are magnificent.

Continue through the middle of the Iron Age fort (Castell Caer Leion) that crowns the summit and start heading downhill, gradually bearing left via a maze of paths towards a wall where you join the main track — the exact point is where the wall bears left away from the track. Bear right along this track, bear left at a junction of tracks and head downhill, going through a metal gate and on to a footpath sign. Cross a track and continue along a path which descends to join another broad track. Keep along this track, by a wall on the left, as it winds downhill below rocky cliffs on the left to join a road at the head of the Sychnant Pass **(C)**. To the right there is a superb view down the pass to the coast and Anglesey.

Cross the road, go through a metal gate opposite, at a public footpath sign, and continue along a grassy path between rocks on the right and woodland on the left. This pleasant, undulating path keeps close to a wall on the left. Climb a metal ladder-stile and bear slightly left to skirt the small shallow lake of Gwern Engan on the left. Past the end of this lake bear right to join a broad path coming in from the left, later picking up a wall on the right and curving right to head downhill to a road.

Follow the road as it curves to the left, and beside a house on the left turn left through a kissing-gate **(D)**. Pass through another kissing-gate, walk along a path enclosed by wire fences, go through another kissing-gate and bear slightly left across a field, crossing a drive and making for a gate. Go through that and continue across a field, passing through a metal gate and on across the next field, later picking up a wire fence and line of trees on the left. Continue, skirting the edge of a wooded hill on the right — there is a fine view from here of Conwy Mountain on the left — to go through a metal kissing-gate. Turn right onto a broad drive which curves to the left and follow it between the buildings of Oakwood Park Hall down to a lane. Turn right for a few yards and at a public footpath sign turn left through a kissing-gate and walk along the right-hand edge of a field, by a hedge on the right, towards the buildings of Conwy straight ahead. Follow the path along the edge of several fields, finally heading across the middle of a field to a kissing-gate. Go through and turn left along the left-hand edge of a field to pass through a kissing-gate by a public footpath sign onto a road **(E)**.

Turn right and follow the road back into Conwy, with striking views ahead of the estuary, castle and medieval walls. Pass through Porth Uchaf, one of the gates in the walls, continue down the street to a road junction and turn right back to the castle.

CALE 1:25 000 or 2½ INCHES to 1 MILE

1 Kilometre

½ mile

37

13 Sarn Helen and the Lledr valley

Start: Dolwyddelan

Distance: 6 miles (9·5 km)

Approximate time: 3 hours

Parking: Parking area near church at Dolwyddelan (alternatively use lay-by just to the west of the village)

Refreshments: Pubs and cafés at Dolwyddelan

Ordnance Survey maps: Landranger 115 (Snowdon) and Outdoor Leisure 16 (Snowdonia — Conwy Valley area)

General description   *Here is a walk in the heart of Snowdonia that has associations with the native Welsh princes. It starts by heading up a lovely enclosed valley, following the line of Sarn Helen, a Roman road, then continues much more steeply through the thick conifers of Gwydyr Forest high above the Lledr valley. The gradual descent into the valley gives open and extensive views, dominated by the rugged grandeur of Moel Siabod in the background and the imposing ruins of Dolwyddelan Castle in the foreground — the latter is in sight for much of the rest of the way and the final leg of the walk passes below its walls.*

The village of Dolwyddelan is spectacularly situated in the Lledr valley about ¾ mile (1·25 km) to the east of the castle and the walk begins at the roadside parking area opposite the small, interesting and largely unrestored sixteenth-century church.

Walk down the road, crossing the river and

The magnificent setting of Dolwyddelan Castle — reputed birthplace of Llywelyn the Great

then the railway, turn right after the railway bridge and follow the road as it bears left and heads uphill. After passing the last of the houses the road narrows to a rough, tarmac track, following the line of the Roman road Sarn Helen, which linked north and south Wales, and proceeding steadily upwards through Cwm Penamnen. Go through a metal gate and continue — this is a most attractive route through the steep-sided valley with forest on the left, crags on the right and the small river gushing over rocks and falls. Pass through another metal gate to enter conifer plantations and now the track levels off.

After it emerges from the plantations a superb view opens up ahead; by a ruined cottage on the left turn right uphill **(A)**, at a public footpath sign, along a wide, grassy path between trees. The path climbs steeply and on entering the conifers bears right for a few yards and then bears left to continue uphill along a broad, stony track. Cross a forestry road and continue steeply upward through the dense, gloomy plantation, turning sharp left near the top and keeping ahead to emerge from the trees **(B)**. Climb a stile, continue uphill for a few yards to go through a gap in a broken wall and ahead is a magnificent view over the Lledr valley dominated by Moel Siabod. Bear right and head downhill across rough grass — there is no obvious path — into a hollow where a discernible path can be seen. Follow this pleasant, green path downhill — after a while it tends to peter out but simply continue in a straight line along the right-hand slopes of the valley, making for a ladder-stile in a wire fence.

Climb the stile, continue downhill along what is now a clear path, and just past a white walker waymark bear right to join a track coming in from the left. Keep along this waymarked track and soon the keep of Dolwyddelan Castle can be seen. The track turns right between ruined buildings, passes through a metal gate and continues gently downhill — at this point there is a particularly outstanding view ahead of the castle backed by Moel Siabod and the winding Lledr can be seen to the left. Turn left through a metal gate to continue downhill into the valley, pass through another metal gate by some trees and 100 yards (91 m) further on turn left off the track across grass — there is no path — heading downhill between rocks. Go through the middle one of three metal gates ahead, continue through another metal gate and on to cross a stream by a footbridge of stone slabs. Turn right to follow a rough path between the stream on the right and trees on the left, joining a track just before reaching the road **(C)**.

Cross over and walk along the narrow lane

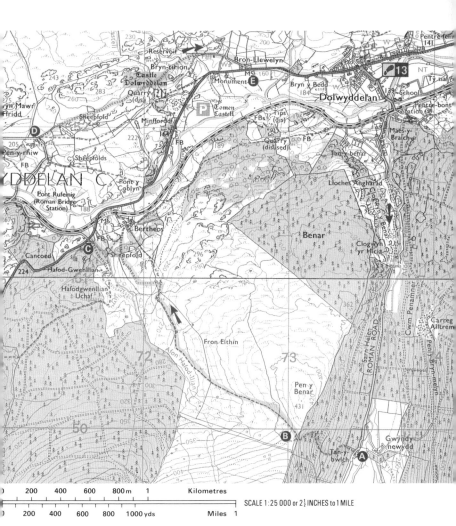

| 200 | 400 | 600 | 800 m | 1 | | Kilometres |
| 200 | 400 | 600 | 800 | 1000 yds | | Miles 1 |

SCALE 1:25 000 or 2½ INCHES to 1 MILE

signposted to Roman Bridge Station, keeping parallel to the railway line and passing the station on the right. Continue uphill below cliffs on the left and follow the lane as it makes a sharp right-hand bend to cross first the railway and then the River Lledr. The lane now winds uphill, passing farm buildings on the left; at a footpath sign turn right **(D)** along a broad track, pass through a metal gate and keep ahead to another metal gate.

Pass through that, continue along the track for another few yards to a fork and here take the right-hand track, following footpath sign directions. Keep in a straight line along this grassy track, with fine views over the valley on the right, and soon the castle keep is seen ahead. Go through a metal gate, head downhill, pass through gateposts and continue below the rocky knoll on the right on which the castle stands. Splendidly situated amidst a wild, rocky landscape and

the reputed birthplace of Llywelyn the Great, Dolwyddelan Castle has a definite aura of romance and mystery. It was one of the principal residences of the princes of Gwynedd and during the English conquest it was occupied by Llywelyn ap Gruffydd, last native prince of Wales, before being captured by Edward I in 1283. At the end of the Middle Ages it fell into ruin and the main surviving parts are the fine twelfth-century keep, which was partially rebuilt in the nineteenth century, and the thirteenth-century west tower.

After passing the castle join a track coming in from the left and follow it downhill, over a bridge and along to a metal gate. Go through and continue along a tree-lined, enclosed track, passing through another metal gate onto a road **(E)**. Turn left for ½ mile (0·75 km) into Dolwyddelan, turning right in the village centre back to the parking area by the church.

14 Aberdaron and the 'Land's End' of North Wales

Start:	Aberdaron
Distance:	7½ miles (12 km). Shorter version 6½ miles (10·5 km)
Approximate time:	4½ hours (4 hours for shorter version)
Parking:	Aberdaron
Refreshments:	Pubs and cafés at Aberdaron, café between Mynydd Mawr and Porth Meudwy
Ordnance Survey maps:	Landranger 123 (Lleyn Peninsula) and Pathfinder 843, SH 12/22/32 (Abersoch & Aberdaron)

General description   *This splendid coastal walk from Aberdaron to Braich y Pwll, the tip of the Lleyn Peninsula, follows in the footsteps of medieval pilgrims on the last stage of their journey to the monastery on Bardsey Island. The views throughout are superb – along the north and south coasts of Lleyn, across to Bardsey Island, and inland over a typical and distinctive Celtic landscape of small, bright green fields separated by hedge-banks, headlands of gorse and heather, and isolated farms. The walk is not strenuous but there are a few places where the coastal path is narrow and slippery and care is needed. It is not recommended in strong winds. The shorter version of the walk omits Braich y Pwll.*

The remote village of Aberdaron is a delightful place. A collection of cottages, with pubs, cafés and shops, clusters above the long sandy beach and up the hill leading into the village, presided over by a small medieval church with a fine Norman doorway – the whole composition in harmony with its surroundings. For the medieval pilgrims on their way to Bardsey Island, Aberdaron was the last stopping place, and the fourteenth-century Y-Gegin Fawr (the Old Kitchen) which gave them food and shelter still appropriately retains a similar function as a café for today's visitors.

Begin by crossing the hump-back bridge over the little river Daron, keep ahead to the beach and turn right to walk along it to Porth Simdde. Climb the steps up the cliff ahead, bearing left at a footpath sign to Porth Meudwy and continuing up the steps to the

cliff top **(A)**, here bearing left again along the narrow coast path. All the way along this well-waymarked path that threads its way between gorse there are splendid views to the left across the bay to Aberdaron and the two tiny islands that lie off the coast.

After passing through a metal kissing-gate drop down to Porth Meudwy **(B)** and continue up steps on the other side, climbing a stile to regain the clifftop. This section of the path is clear and easy to follow but as it is also narrow and rather worn and crumbly in places care is needed. Continue above a succession of steep-sided coves, negotiating some rocks at one point, climb a stile, and after passing the last of the series of coves (Hen Borth) take the right-hand higher path at a fork, keeping parallel to a wall on the left a little way ahead. (Do not take the slightly lower path nearer the cliff edge.) Head across the breezy, open grassland of the headland of Pen y Cil towards the rocks ahead – the exact path is rather unclear at this point as there is a proliferation of sheep-tracks but keep in a straight line towards the rocks. On reaching the top of the cliffs there is a sheer

drop below and the first view of Bardsey Island across the treacherous waters of Bardsey Sound.

Turn right to climb through the rocks to the top of the headland, making towards the cairn which marks the summit of Pen y Cil, a superb viewpoint (C). Continue past the cairn and the National Trust plaque to pick up a clear, broad path, following it to a ladder-stile. Climb the stile, turn left to a metal gate and footpath sign — this section of the route is waymarked by finger-posts with a cross and arrow — go through the gate and continue along the right-hand edge of a field, by a bank and wire fence on the right, in the direction of the prominent hill of Mynydd Mawr (Big Mountain). Climb a ladder-stile to enter the National Trust property of Bychestyn and continue by a wall and wire fence on the right, passing through a metal gate and keeping ahead along a grassy path to a T-junction by a finger-post.

Here turn right along a broad, enclosed track to the next finger-post and turn left along another track, which curves to the left and continues to a metal gate. Go through, climb the ladder-stile a short distance ahead and then turn right, following the waymarked directions to the top left-hand corner of the field to go through another metal gate. Now turn left, making towards a metal gate, go through that and continue along the edge of a field to pass through another metal gate. Keep ahead, at first by a bank on the left and later joining a bank on the right, to follow a track up to a metal gate onto a lane (D).

At this point those wishing to do only the shorter version of the walk, omitting Braich y Pwll and Mynydd Mawr, can turn right, following the main route after (D) overleaf.

Turn left along the lane, passing over a cattle-grid to a waymark just before the lane bends to the right. Here bear slightly left along a broad track and bear right at a finger-post onto a path which heads uphill between rocks and bracken over the headland of Braich y Pwll, the 'Land's End' of North Wales – a lovely, wild, romantic spot, totally uncommercialised and with superb views of Bardsey Island. On reaching a concrete platform, site of a wartime radar station, turn right to climb a flight of steps that leads to the summit of Mynydd Mawr **(E)**, a magnificent viewpoint which overlooks the whole length of the Lleyn Peninsula, the view including the distant mountains of Snowdonia, Cardigan and Caernarfon bays and, in exceptionally clear conditions, the Wicklow Mountains of Ireland. Here there is a car park, a coastguard station, and nearby the remains of prehistoric hut circles.

Continue along a concrete road which heads downhill, first bending sharply to the right, then bending equally sharply to the left, and where it bends to the right again keep ahead along a faint but discernible path which heads down to a farm. Look out for a small wooden gate below on the right; go through it and continue between the farm buildings and along the tarmac drive ahead to come out onto a lane just a few yards to the left of the earlier route **(D)**.

Turn left along the lane (those on the shorter version of the walk will have turned right along it) for nearly ½ mile (0·75 km). Just past a public footpath sign and where the lane bends to the left bear right **(F)** along a track in front of a rather strategically placed café, walk past a farm, pass through two metal gates in quick succession and continue across a field. Go through a narrow metal gate at the far end of the field, keep straight ahead across the next field to climb a ladder-stile, and continue to another small metal gate. Go through that, descend some steps and turn right along a track which leads down to a lane. Turn right along the lane for a few yards to a footpath sign; here turn left up some steps to walk along a raised bank, descending steps again at the far end onto another lane.

Turn right towards a farm (Tir Glyw), then turn left along a track, passing to the left of the farm buildings and continuing to the end of a field. Here follow a path which heads downhill and go through a metal kissing-gate. Turn left, cross a stream, climb a low fence and continue along a grassy path, soon bearing right to join a broad track which heads down through a narrow valley to Porth Meudwy **(B)**. Turn left to rejoin the coast path and the outward route and retrace your steps to Aberdaron.

Aberdaron from the coast path

15 Yr Eifl

Start:	Forestry Commission car park ½ mile (0·75 km) north of Llithfaen
Distance:	4 miles (6·5 km)
Approximate time:	3 hours
Parking:	Forestry Commission car park
Refreshments:	None
Ordnance Survey maps:	Landranger 123 (Lleyn Peninsula) and Pathfinder 801, SH 34/44 (Llanaelhaearn)

General description *Despite the short distance and although only a modest height of 1,850 feet (564 m) is reached, this is quite a strenuous walk with a fair amount of climbing across terrain similar to that in the higher mountain country of Snowdonia, and with some rough going in places. Yr Eifl, though incorrectly anglicised to 'the Rivals', means 'the Forks' and comprises three neighbouring peaks that rise above the north coast of the Lleyn Peninsula. They are a*

prominent landmark for many miles and from them the views up and down the length of Lleyn, across the water to Anglesey and along the western edge of Snowdonia are superb. Do not attempt this walk in misty conditions as this would make route finding between the summits very difficult.

From the car park turn right along the lane for a short distance and at a bridleway sign turn sharp left onto a broad track which heads steadily uphill to a pass (Bwlch yr Eifl) between the western and central peaks of Yr Eifl. From here there are fine views to the left down the valley of Nant Gwrtheyrn to the coast. At the top of the pass an even grander view unfolds ahead along the Lleyn coast, with Anglesey and the mountains of Snowdonia on the horizon. At this point, opposite a metal gate and a track leading up to a transmitting station on the western peak, turn right (**A**) onto a broad, clear path that heads steadily uphill to the central one of the three peaks, which at 1,850 feet (564 m) is also the highest. The path winds upwards between heather, becomes considerably narrower and crosses other paths, heading continually towards the summit that looms in front. On reaching the stones that crown the summit it veers first left and later right, becomes faint in places and some scrambling is needed, though this is made easy because

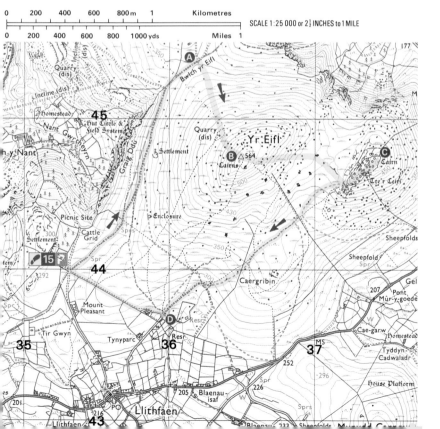

SCALE 1:25 000 or 2½ INCHES to 1 MILE

The Iron Age fort of Tre'r Ceiri crowns one of the three peaks of Yr Eifl

the rock slabs are so large. The summit is marked by a large cairn, shelter and triangulation pillar **(B)**, from where there is a magnificent panoramic view up and down the north and south coasts of the Lleyn Peninsula, along the western edge of Snowdonia and across to Anglesey – one of the finest viewpoints in Wales.

Now make for the third peak which can be clearly seen to the east, 1,591 feet (485 m) high and crowned by the ramparts of its Iron Age fort. Head towards it, in a direction slightly to the left of the previous one, following a narrow but reasonably discernible path that heads downhill, bearing slightly to the left all the time. Where the path forks just below the summit of the central peak continue along the left-hand path (even though the right-hand one looks the clearer and more important), at one stage passing below some huge boulders on the left before bearing right away from them quite steeply downhill into the valley between the two peaks. From here continue across a flat area of rough grass, which is likely to be boggy and at times the path almost disappears, but keep in a straight line, making for a path that can be seen ahead snaking up the hillside.

After picking up this path, which soon starts to climb, bear right and then left through a gap in the outer walls of the Iron Age fort of Tre'r Ceiri, which occupies the summit of the hill and covers an area of five acres. Its remains are among the most substantial and impressive in Wales – a series of defensive walls within which are a large number of hut circles. Follow a path more steeply now between rocks, go through another gap in the walls and turn left up to the summit cairn **(C)**, passing the remains of many of the hut circles on the way. From here there is another magnificent panoramic view – the village of Llanaelhaearn lies immediately below and you can clearly see from here how the north face of the western peak has been eaten into by quarrying activities.

Retrace your steps to where you entered the outer walls of the fort and turn left to follow a downhill path through the valley between the central and eastern peaks. Bear slightly right on joining a broader path and at the next fork take the narrower right-hand path which continues down to a wall. Climb a metal ladder-stile, just to the right of a gate, and continue along a clear path which as it descends reveals more fine views in front of the coastlines and the rolling hills of Lleyn, with the village of Llithfaen immediately ahead.

Climb a ladder-stile, continue towards the village and about 200 yards (183 m) before the nearest house bear right **(D)** onto a path which soon crosses a track and heads over open grassland towards another house. Turn right along a track in front of the house and follow it back to the starting point, keeping by a wall on the left all the way.

6 Moelfre, Din Lligwy and Yr Arwydd

Start:	Moelfre
Distance:	10 miles (16 km)
Approximate time:	5½ hours
Parking:	Moelfre
Refreshments:	Pubs and cafés at Moelfre, pub about ⅓ mile (0·6 km) north-west of Brynrefail
Ordnance Survey maps:	Landranger 114 (Anglesey) and Pathfinder 735, SH 48/58 (Red Wharf Bay)

General description *This lengthy but fairly flat and undemanding walk on the east coast of Anglesey, mostly along quiet lanes and field and coast paths, includes a series of historic sites and a wide variety of scenery. The historic attractions include a prehistoric burial chamber, remains of a fourth-century fortified village, ruins of a twelfth-century chapel and a medieval church; the scenery takes in fields and woodland, open moorland, Anglesey's highest point and a magnificent stretch of coastline above some of the finest sandy beaches in the country.*

Refer to map overleaf.

Start at the harbour in the small resort and fishing village of Moelfre. Walk up the hill away from the harbour and take the first road on the right. Follow it past modern housing, turn left in front of the community centre **(A)** and continue along a concrete farm drive. Where the drive bends to the right keep ahead along a hedge-lined track, go through a kissing-gate and continue along the right-hand edge of a field, by a broken wall on the right. At the end of the wall turn right and head across a field, bearing slightly left to go through a kissing-gate by a yellow waymark. Continue straight across the next field, parallel to a stream on the left and keeping to the left of a low wall and line of trees, to another kissing-gate. Go through that, cross the stream and follow the direction of a waymark to the left through a metal gate. Turn right between farm buildings, pass through another metal gate and continue along a track, through a kissing-gate and over some steps in a wall to a road.

Turn right and follow the road up to a roundabout **(B)**; here turn right along a lane signposted to Din Lligwy. Now follows the remarkable series of Lligwy historic monuments, all within a short distance of each other. After about ½ mile (0·75 km) a kissing-gate on the left leads to Lligwy Burial Chamber, erected in the later Neolithic period (2500 – 2000 BC), for the communal burial of the dead and probably originally covered by a mound of earth or stones. Continue along the lane, with fine views to the right over the sea to Snowdonia and the Great Orme, and a little further on go through another kissing-gate on the left, at a sign for Din Lligwy and Hen Capel **(C)**. Go down some steps and walk along the left-hand edge of a field, by a wall and wire fence on the left, bearing left at the end of the field and following signs to Din Lligwy into the next field. Bear right, passing through two metal gates in quick succession, to enter woodland and climb some steps to reach the enclosure containing the remains of Din Lligwy. This highly atmospheric site was a fortified village built by the natives of Anglesey in the latter part of the Roman occupation of Wales. It comprises a number of round and rectangular huts enclosed within a polygonal defensive wall and was principally occupied during the fourth century AD. Retrace your steps and follow signs across to the ruins of Hen Capel Lligwy, a twelfth-century chapel with later additions, from which there is a superb view of the sweeping sandy expanse of Traeth Lligwy.

Return to the lane and keep along it downhill to a crossroads **(D)**. Turn left along another lane for ¼ mile (0·5 km) and just after crossing a stream and rounding a bend to the right turn left **(E)** at a sign for a farm and caravan site, go through some white gates and walk along a drive, passing a house on the right. Just past the house climb some

Hen Capel Lligwy — one of the remarkable series of Lligwy historic monuments on the east coast of Anglesey

steps on the right and continue along a narrow path by the right-hand edge of woodland. After a short distance this joins a track: turn right along it and where the track turns right keep ahead through a caravan site, turn left to cross a stream and immediately turn right along another narrow woodland path. Head uphill and follow a winding path across a small area of rocky heathland, bearing right on joining a broad track and keeping along it up to a road (**F**). Cross over and continue for nearly ¾ mile (1·25 km) along the narrow lane opposite, to a T-junction (**G**).

Turn left along the road, which soon bends to the right, and at this point a brief detour to the left brings you to the lovely, simple, medieval church of St Michael's,

Penrhoslligwy. Continue along the road for just over ¼ mile (0·5 km), climbing steadily, and just after the road flattens out turn sharply to the right along a broad, stony, uphill track (**H**). Soon the track flattens out; continue along it to the farm buildings of Tyn y Mynydd. Alternatively, turn left onto one of the permissive paths which lead up through heather and rocks to the modest summit of Yr Arwydd — an easy, short and not very strenuous climb which, in such a flat landscape, rewards you with a magnificent panoramic view over the whole of Anglesey, the Menai Strait, the Lleyn Peninsula, the Great Orme and the mountains of Snowdonia.

At the farm (**J**) turn right (or continue straight on if descending from Yr Arwydd)

long a track between buildings and go through a metal gate with a yellow waymark. Continue, passing to the right of a house, climb a stone stile in a wall on the right and turn left along the left-hand edge of a field to climb a waymarked stile. The next part of the route is well waymarked. Keep ahead to another waymark, picking up and keeping by a wire fence on the right, continue in a straight line and later bear slightly left away from the fence to pass through a metal gate and on to a stile a few yards ahead. Climb it, cross a footbridge over a ditch, climb another stile and continue along the edge of a rather boggy area of trees and gorse on the right, bearing slightly right to climb a stile.

Now follow a path downhill between wire fences across an area of gorse and heather to a ladder-stile. Climb it, bear right to keep by an outcrop of rocks and a wire fence on the right, heading down to climb another ladder-stile. Continue, at first keeping by a wire fence on the right and later bearing slightly left away from it to go through a gap at the end of a field. Keeping by a wall and line of trees on the right, pass through another gap and continue, ascending to reach another ladder-stile half-hidden among trees. Climb it

SCALE 1:25 000 or 2½ INCHES to 1 MILE

1 Kilometre

½ mile

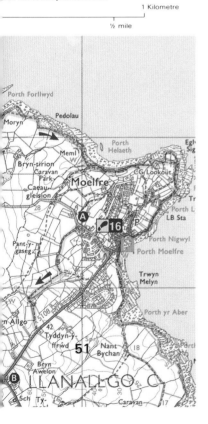

and walk through a small area of woodland, briefly descending and dropping down steps to continue in the same direction along the right-hand edge of a field. In the bottom corner of the field look out for a stone stile; climb it and keep ahead to descend some steps to a lane. Turn left and walk past a chapel, down a ramp and onto the main road at Brynrefail (**K**).

Turn left along the road and soon a kissing-gate on the right leads to the Morris Memorial, a monument to three brothers who were born in the locality in the eighteenth century and were renowned for their wide range of intellectual and scientific activities. Continue along the road as far as the Pilot Boat Inn (**L**) and in front of it turn right through a kissing-gate at a public footpath sign. Walk along the right-hand edge of a field, by a low wall and wire fence on the right – below to the left is the inlet of Traeth Dulas. Turn right over a ladder-stile, turn left along the edge of the next field, this time with a wall and wire fence on the left, and follow the field edge round to the right to turn left over a ladder-stile. Continue along an uphill track to climb another ladder-stile, keep along the right-hand edge of a smooth, broad, grassy headland, with outcrops of rock covered with gorse to the left, and descend gently to a ladder-stile.

Climb it, keep ahead to a waymark and continue past it, bearing slightly right and heading downhill. Go through a gap between bushes and continue along the right-hand edge of the grassy headland, below a partially wooded bank on the right, to go through a kissing-gate beside a cottage. Keep by the side of the cottage, turn right along the edge of the garden, go up some steps and climb a stile onto a lane. Turn left down the lane, bearing slightly right at a public footpath sign along an enclosed, tree-lined track which bends to the left at another public footpath sign. After this the track becomes a narrow, hedge-lined path; follow it to the coast above the glorious beach of Traeth yr Ora (**M**).

Turn right to follow the coast path back to Moelfre – with superb views of the mainland and the mass of Snowdonia peaks on the skyline ahead for much of the way and glimpses of Yr Arwydd to the right – along the edge of the magnificent expanses of sand at Traeth yr Ora and Traeth Lligwy. The route is easy to follow and well waymarked. It keeps along low cliffs most of the way, goes up and down steps several times, negotiates stiles and kissing-gates and crosses an area of dunes at Traeth Lligwy. On approaching the houses of Moelfre the path goes through a caravan site and follows the waymarks around the headland, passing a coastguard lookout station and finally the lifeboat station before reaching the harbour.

17 Dyffryn Ardudwy and Pont-Scethin

Start: Dyffryn Ardudwy

Distance: 8 miles (12·75 km)

Approximate time: 4½ hours

Parking: Dyffryn Ardudwy

Refreshments: Café at Dyffryn Ardudwy

Ordnance Survey maps: Landranger 124 (Dolgellau) and Outdoor Leisure 18 (Snowdonia – Harlech & Bala areas)

General description *For those who want to enjoy a long walk in open, wild, remote surroundings, but without strenuous ascents or challenging and difficult paths, this route in the southern Rhinogs is ideal. The going is easy throughout, the paths are clear and firm – apart from a few boggy sections in the middle part of the walk – and the scenery is superb. Near the end are three additional bonuses: some delightful woodland, fine coastal views and two prehistoric burial chambers.*

From the car park turn left up to the main road, cross over and take the uphill lane opposite, turning right at a junction, at a public footpath sign, along a track (**A**). Where the track ends continue along a road which bears left and peters out into a track again before continuing towards farm buildings. Just before reaching the farm turn right at a footpath sign, pass through two metal gates in quick succession, continue through a third and then bear slightly left along a walled, grassy track. At a junction of tracks turn right along the right-hand edge of a field, a route clearly marked with yellow arrows and by a wall and line of trees on the right, passing through a kissing-gate and continuing along the left-hand edge of the next field, this time with the wall on the left to climb a ladder-stile onto a lane (**B**).

Turn left along this lane, passing through an impressive avenue of trees which was once part of the drive of Cors y Gedol Hall, curving right and left around the boundary wall of the hall and then turning right to continue in the same direction as before. Ahead are impressive views of the southern Rhinogs. Where the lane ends go through a metal gate where a notice says 'No vehicles beyond this gate' and keep ahead along a broad, walled track, passing through a series of gates to continue through the wild, open,

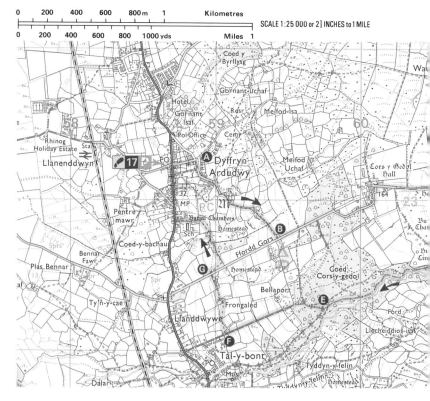

SCALE 1:25 000 or 2½ INCHES to 1 MILE

onely, barren terrain of the valley of the Afon Ysgethin. After the walls on both sides finish continue along the track for a short distance and opposite a small plantation over to the left, and at a yellow waymark, bear right to follow a grassy path across moorland, heading down to Pont-Scethin (**C**). This old pack-horse bridge was once used by drovers on their way to England and, although difficult to believe in such a remote spot, it was later used by mail coaches travelling between London and Harlech.

Cross the bridge and turn right to follow a faint but waymarked path across a boggy area — there are some boardwalks here — to reach a standing stone. Here turn right along a grassy track and follow it for 2 miles (3·25 km) through this austere but beautiful landscape, passing Llyn Erddyn and going through a succession of metal gates. At a T-junction of tracks turn right down a broad, walled track which curves left to a gate. Go through it and continue down a tarmac track which bears right over Pont Fadog (**D**), another old pack-horse bridge over the Afon Ysgethin. Go through a gate at the far end of the bridge, bear left uphill, and opposite a house on the right bear left, at a footpath sign, along a path which heads through the delightful, steep-sided woodland of Coed Cors-y-gedol above the river. This section of

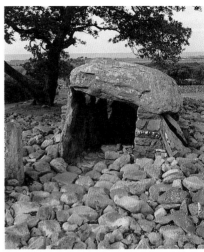

A prehistoric burial chamber near Dyffryn Ardudwy

the walk is in striking contrast to the earlier treeless wilderness. Continue by the river — the path later widens to become a track — and at a fork bear right (**E**) away from the river, following the broader of two tracks, bearing right again at the next fork a few yards ahead. Soon look out for a path on the left and walk along it to cross a footbridge

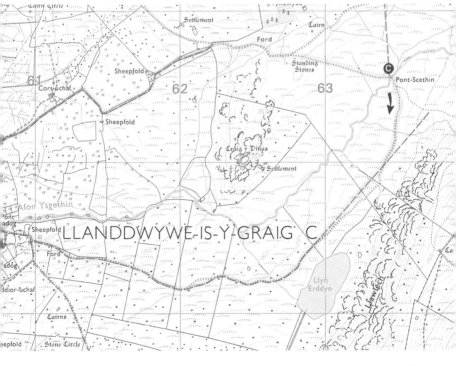

The view across Cardigan Bay to the Lleyn Peninsula from the lonely valley of the Afon Ysgethin

over a stream and continue to the edge of the woods.

Climb some steps, go through a metal gate and, with a glorious view over Cardigan Bay ahead, keep ahead to join a straight, tarmac farm road. Follow this road gently downhill for just over ¼ mile (0·5 km), passing through a gate and continuing as far as a stepped stile on the right (F). Climb it and bear right to a metal gate and yellow waymark a few yards ahead on the left. Go through the gate and up some steps across a very broad wall, go down steps on the other side and continue along the edge of a field, by a wall on the left. Climb more steps over another broad wall and continue along the right-hand edge of the next field, now with the wall on the right, passing through a metal

gate. Bear right to join a farm track and follow it through several gates down to a lane (G). Cross over, go through the gate opposite and bear right across a field towards its top edge. Continue along the edge of the field, by a wall on the right, climb a stone stile to enter woodland, walk through the wood and at the far end keep ahead across a field, bearing left to pass through a gate. Now continue by a wall on the left – the boundary wall of the Dyffryn Burial Chambers, which date from the Neolithic period.

Keep ahead past the burial chambers, go through a gate and continue, by a wall on the left and houses on the right, to go through another gate onto the main road. Turn right and walk through the village back to the car park.

18 Tal-y-fan

Start:	Roewen
Distance:	7 miles (11·25 km)
Approximate time:	4 hours
Parking:	Roadside parking at lower end of Roewen village
Refreshments:	Pub and café at Roewen
Ordnance Survey maps:	Landranger 115 (Snowdon) and Outdoor Leisure 16 (Snowdonia – Conwy Valley area)

General description *Tal-y-fan is the most north-easterly of the Carneddau peaks, overlooking Conwy and the coast and separated from the rest of the range by the Bwlch y Ddeufaen pass. At just 2,000 feet (610 m) it is also the lowest mountain in Snowdonia. It is the ideal introduction for those who want to climb a mountain without too much effort and especially for anyone inexperienced and nervous of tackling the more challenging ascents. This is also a walk of considerable historic interest, initially following the line of a Roman road, also passing a number of prehistoric monuments and visiting a tiny medieval church in a lovely remote setting. Despite its relative ease this is a walk to be attempted only in good weather, as in misty conditions route finding, especially in the middle section between the summit of Tal-y-fan and Llangelynin, could be difficult without experience in using a compass.*

Refer to map overleaf.

The village of Roewen, on the western side of the Conwy Valley, makes an attractive starting point for the walk. Begin by walking through the village, passing the pub on the right, and turn right at the first road junction **(A)**.

Follow a lane which heads uphill by houses, becoming narrower and steeper, and which descends briefly before climbing again between trees, degenerating into a rough track after passing a youth hostel. Continue uphill along this pleasant, enclosed track, which follows the line of a Roman road which ran between the forts of Canovium (Caerhun) in the Conwy Valley and Segontium (Caernarfon) via the Bwlch y Ddeufaen pass, part of a longer route linking Chester and Caernarfon. Go through a metal gate and continue, now less steeply, passing the Maen-y-Bardd (Bard's Stone) burial chamber which is on the right, then a standing stone a little further on (on the other wide of the wall on the left) and, after going through two metal gates in quick succession, another standing stone a little further ahead on the right. It is probably from these two stones that the pass gets its name as Bwlch y Ddeufaen means 'the Pass of Two Stones'. Continue through another metal gate, shortly joining a tarmac lane which comes in from the left.

Ahead the lane continues through the pass, but about 100 yards (91 m) after joining this lane turn right **(B)** over a ladder-stile and head straight up the hill in front along a path through gorse bushes to a white walker waymark, here bearing right to a ladder-stile. Climb it and continue steadily uphill, following white walker marker-posts and drawing close to and keeping parallel to a wall on the right. Turn right over a ladder-stile in that wall, immediately turn left and head up to another marker-post, bearing away from the wall and continuing between rocks and heather to reach another ladder-stile **(C)**.

Climb it and turn right for a ½-mile (0·75 km) detour from the main route to the summit. Follow a path that heads up between boulders and heather, keeping parallel to a wall on the right, the path becoming increasingly steep and rocky towards the summit of Tal-y-fan; the summit cairn is just on the other side of the wall and can be reached by a stile **(D)**. The magnificent all-round view from here gives the best of both worlds – coast and mountains – and takes in the Conwy Valley, Conwy town and castle, Conwy Mountain, Llandudno and the Great Orme, the Clwydian Hills, the North Wales coast, Anglesey and the Carneddau range.

Roewen village

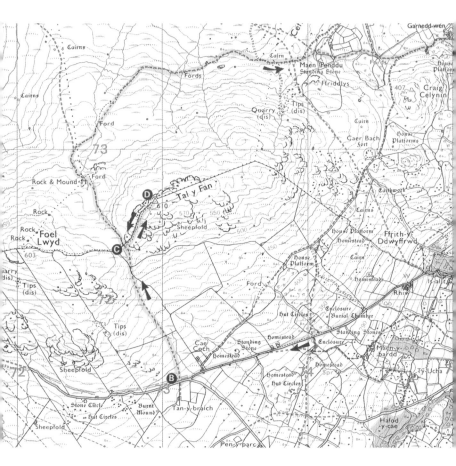

The lovely, isolated Llangelynin Old Church below the heights of Tal-y-fan

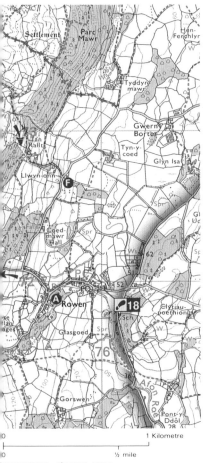

SCALE 1:25 000 or 2½ INCHES to 1 MILE

crosses several small streams that tumble down from the slopes of Tal-y-fan. Pass to the right of the burial chamber of Maen-Penddu and continue to a junction of paths. Here bear slightly right — again route finding can be somewhat confusing because of the multitude of paths — heading gently uphill again to go over a shallow pass. On joining a grassy track coming in from the right keep ahead for about 100 yards (91 m) to a large, isolated boulder on the right. In front there is a superb view over the Conwy Valley to the Clwydian Hills on the horizon. Turn half-right along a narrow, boggy path heading towards a wall, and just before reaching it bear left and continue downhill, keeping parallel to this wall on the right. As you descend there is a fine view to the left over Conwy, the estuary and the Great Orme, and the strategic importance of Conwy Castle can be appreciated.

Later pick up and keep by a wall on the left for a while, continuing more or less in a straight line downhill, bearing right to pass through a wall gap and on to join a grassy track. Keep ahead along this track, passing through two metal gates in quick succession, and continue along an enclosed, downhill track. Ahead is Llangelynin Old Church, an unpretentious and unspoilt medieval church in a lovely remote setting, cradled by hills and completely in harmony with its surroundings. Before reaching the church and opposite a ladder-stile on the left turn right (**E**), by a wall on the left, to a stile and gate a few yards ahead. Climb the stile (a strange stone- and ladder-stile) and continue roughly parallel with a wall on the right, but bearing slightly left away from it to climb the left-hand one of two ladder-stiles in front. From here there is a superb view looking down the Conwy Valley with Roewen immediately below.

Head downhill by a low wall on the right — the wall later peters out — passing to the left of a ruined house. Soon afterwards turn right through a gap into a field, head towards the house and veer left in front of it to pick up a faint path that heads downhill, by an embankment on the right, looking out for a ladder-stile perched somewhat incongruously between two small parallel streams. Climb it, keep ahead for a few yards and then bear left along a broad, downhill track between trees, soon picking up and keeping by a wire fence on the left. Just after passing a house below on the left turn left and head down to a metal gate. Go through and turn right through another metal gate by the side of a farmhouse.

Continue along a drive which soon turns left, heads downhill and curves right to a lane (**F**). Bear right along the lane for ½ mile (0·75 km), heading up to a T-junction to rejoin the outward route. Turn left and retrace your steps to Roewen.

Return to the ladder-stile at (**C**) and turn right along a path that initially skirts the base of rocks on the right and then continues ahead across heather. From now on the path is not very clear and route finding can be confusing because of the number of sheep tracks, but the path is recognisable most of the time and keeps in a slightly north-westerly direction, just above a shallow, boggy valley on the left and heading gently downhill. Cross the stream on the left where it bears right and continue, soon picking up a reasonably clear, wide, grassy path which bears right and passes to the left of a mound with a collection of spiky rocks. The summit of Tal-y-fan is now to the right. Continue along this path — it peters out now and then — in a north-easterly direction, recrossing the stream, on the other side of which there is again a recognisable path.

Keep to the right of a circular enclosure, heading gently downhill and curving slightly to the right to continue, now in an easterly direction. The path is boggy in places and

19 Trefriw, Llyn Geirionydd and Llyn Crafnant

Start:	Trefriw
Distance:	8 miles (12·75 km). Shorter version 7 miles (11·25 km)
Approximate time:	4 hours (3 ½ hours for shorter version)
Parking:	Trefriw
Refreshments:	Pubs and cafés at Trefriw, café by Llyn Crafnant for those doing the shorter walk
Ordnance Survey maps:	Landranger 115 (Snowdon) and Outdoor Leisure 16 (Snowdonia – Conwy Valley area)

General description *On their eastern flanks the Carneddau drop steeply to the broad valley of the River Conwy and in the narrow side valleys that cut into the range a number of reservoirs have been constructed. They blend in with their surroundings so well that it is difficult to tell them from natural lakes. This fairly undemanding walk takes in two of these lakes as well as areas of conifer forest and deciduous woodland, and provides constantly outstanding views over both the mountains and the Conwy Valley.*

Trefriw occupies a fine situation below the wooded slopes of the Carneddau on the western side of the Conwy Valley and is noted for its woollen-mill where visitors can watch the various stages in the production of tweeds and tapestries. Just to the north of the village is the Victorian spa of Trefriw Wells.

From the car park walk up to the woollen-mill and turn left along the road. Take the first turning on the right along an uphill lane, following it as it curves to the left past houses. Just before it bends to the right turn left along another narrow uphill lane, and where that lane bends sharply to the left keep ahead along a path which climbs up to another narrow lane. Turn right for a few yards and at a public footpath sign turn left **(A)** along a narrow path which leads up to a stile. Climb over and continue along a delightful path which winds through rocks and trees along the side of the Crafnant valley, keeping high above the river. Ahead grand views soon open up over the Carneddau. Go through a metal gate and continue, bearing right and following the right-hand edge of a wall to pass through a wooden gate. Keep ahead, bearing right over a stream and continuing between gorse bushes, over two ladder-stiles and by a stream and wire fence on the right to join the road by Llyn Geirionydd.

Climb a stile and turn right **(B)** across the end of the lake. Over to the right is a monument to a sixth-century Welsh poet called Taliesen who is believed to have lived near here. Follow the edge of the lake round to the left, climb a stile and continue along a wooded path. This hugs the edge of the lake and is fairly clear but narrow, rocky and quite difficult in places because of the encroaching conifers. At the far end of the lake climb a stile, keep ahead along a broad, uphill track, and just before it bends to the right turn right **(C)** onto a narrow, uphill path through thick conifers. Recross the track and keep ahead, crossing the track again and continuing uphill. A forestry road is joined for about 30 yards (27 m); where it bends sharply to the right keep ahead along another narrow path which soon levels out and starts to descend. Climb a stile and, with a fine view ahead over the lovely Llyn Crafnant, head downhill, bearing left to a ladder-stile and climbing it to join the lane alongside the lake **(D)**.

*At this point those wishing to do only the shorter version of the walk can turn right along the lane to rejoin the main route at **(F)** below. This way has pleasant views over the lake and passes the café by the lakeshore.*

Turn left and follow the lane for nearly ¾ mile (1·25 km). After passing through gateposts turn right **(E)** along a broad track, go through a gate, turn right over a footbridge, pass through a metal gate immediately in front and continue towards the end of the lake. Turn left over a stile by some trees and then turn right to follow a forest track along the edge of Llyn Crafnant to the far end, here curving right and passing another monument to rejoin the lane **(F)**.

Turn left (those on the shorter version continue) along the lane for 1½ miles (2·5 km) through very attractive woodland and by the River Crafnant for most of the time. Where the river bends right away from the lane turn sharp right **(G)** along a track,

almost doubling back, cross the river and immediately turn sharp left, doubling back again, for a few yards before turning right to go up some steps and through a wooden gate. Head across the field, pass through a gate and continue along a pleasantly wooded, undulating path which keeps roughly parallel with the river on the left. Ahead there are superb views over the Conwy Valley.

Soon the houses of Trefriw can be seen. Go through a kissing-gate and continue along the road to a T-junction. Turn left to cross the river, take the first turning on the right, bear right at a junction and turn right again at a crossroads to recross the river and return to the starting point.

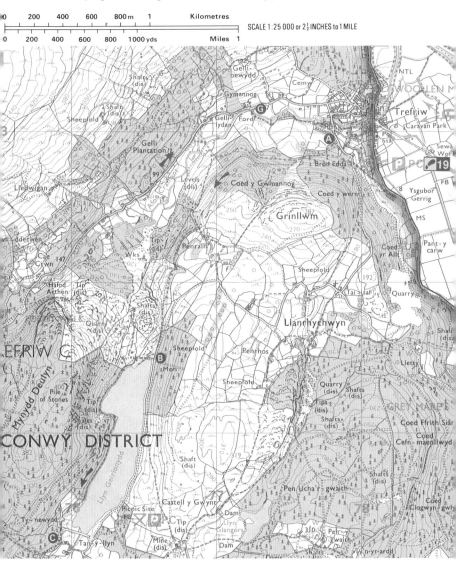

SCALE 1:25 000 or 2½ INCHES to 1 MILE

20 Aberdovey, Happy Valley and the Bearded Lake

Start:	Aberdovey
Distance:	8 miles (12·75 km)
Approximate time:	4 hours
Parking:	Aberdovey
Refreshments:	Pubs, restaurants and cafés at Aberdovey
Ordnance Survey maps:	Landranger 135 (Aberystwyth) and Outdoor Leisure 23 (Snowdonia — Cadair Idris area)

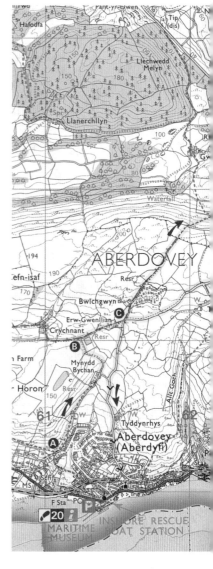

General description *From the shores of the Dovey estuary the route climbs out of the valley and descends by field paths and tracks into the quiet, beautiful Cwm Maethlon, renamed the Happy Valley by delighted Victorian visitors. It then continues along to the reedy, mysterious-looking waters of Llyn Barfog (the Bearded Lake) before returning to Aberdovey via a splendid, panoramic ridge walk. The views over the Dovey estuary and the great sweep of Cardigan Bay on this latter part of the walk are magnificent — the whole of the west coast of Wales, from the tip of the Lleyn Peninsula to St David's Head in Pembrokeshire, can be seen.*

Some attractive Georgian buildings and a harbour are a reminder that Aberdovey was once a busy, flourishing port and fishing village before its later rise in the Victorian era as a seaside resort. It is still a bustling, popular holiday resort, boasting a long, sandy beach and a good range of shops, pubs, cafés, hotels and restaurants.

Start on the seafront at the tourist information centre and with your back to the estuary turn right towards the church and then left up Copperhill Street. Pass under the railway bridge and just after passing Copperhill Walk on the right turn sharp left along an uphill, winding, tarmac path which gives fine views to the left over the town and estuary. At a path junction turn sharp right along another uphill, winding, tarmac path; after climbing some steps this widens into a track, which in turn, after passing a row of bungalows on the left, becomes a lane. Keep ahead to a public footpath sign and ladder-stile (**A**).

Climb the stile and turn right along a narrow and sometimes overgrown path through bracken, above houses on the right; later the path becomes hedge-lined and continues, passing a barn on the right, to a footpath sign. Keep ahead along an uphill track, go through a metal gate and pass to the left of a small reservoir to reach a T-junction (**B**). Turn right, go through another metal gate and continue — passing a house on the right — to a lane and meeting of tracks (**C**).

Turn left along an uphill tarmac track to a gate. Go through, keep ahead to pass through another metal gate and continue uphill along an enclosed track to emerge into open country with fine panoramic views. Keep along the left-hand edge of a field, by a

0   200   400   600   800 m   1   Kilometres

0   200   400   600   800   1000 yds   Miles 1

SCALE 1:25 000 or 2½ INCHES to 1 MILE

wire fence on the left, go through the left-hand one of a pair of metal gates and continue, now with a wire fence on the right, to go through another metal gate. Walk straight across the field ahead – there are lovely views from here of the coast to the left and Happy Valley in front – turning half-right at a fence corner and heading downhill into the valley. Near the bottom of the field bear right along a discernible grassy path, above a steam on the left, to a metal gate. Go through it and continue downhill, by a wire fence on the left and later along the edge of woodland, passing through another metal gate to enter the wood and curving left and then right to join the small stream of Afon Dyffryn-gwyn.

Cross the footbridge over the stream on the left, keep ahead to climb a stile and, passing to the right of the buildings of Dyffryn-gwyn, walk along a farm track to a road (D). Turn right along the road for ½ mile (0·75 km), heading uphill to a car park; here turn right (E) through a metal gate and continue along a winding, waymarked track up to Tyddyn-y-briddell. Turn left in front of the farm buildings to climb a ladder-stile to the right of a metal gate and continue along a track to another ladder-stile. Climb it and shortly afterwards, at a footpath sign, bear right off the track along an uphill path, making for a ladder-stile in the wall ahead. Climb that, continue more gently uphill to climb yet another ladder-stile and ahead are the lonely, reedy, mysterious-looking waters of Llyn Barfog (the Bearded Lake), perhaps not surprisingly rich in folklore and Arthurian legends – according to one of these King Arthur killed a monster who lived in the lake.

Walk towards the lake and turn right along a grassy track **(F)**, from which there is a magnificent view ahead across the Dovey valley to Plynlimon and the Cambrian mountains of mid Wales. At a junction of tracks turn right to a ladder-stile; climb it and head gently uphill to join and keep by a wall on the left. Climb another ladder-stile and continue downhill, by a wire fence on the right, curving right to a cottage. At a footpath sign in front of the cottage bear left **(G)** through a metal gate and head up to another metal gate.

Go through it and follow the narrow lane ahead along the ridge for 2 miles (3·25 km) to the junction of the lane and several tracks which was passed earlier **(C)**. This is a superb high-level route, giving the finest views of the entire walk – to the right over the Happy Valley and ahead the most magnificent panorama over the coast, taking in the whole sweep of Cardigan Bay from the Lleyn Peninsula in the north to St David's Head in Pembrokeshire in the south.

At the junction keep along the lane as it turns left and follow it downhill for another ¾ mile (1·25 km) into Aberdovey, with fine views ahead all the time over the town and estuary. Turn sharp right at a T-junction, continue downhill, passing the church on the left, and turn left back to the seafront.

The mysterious-looking waters of Llyn Barfog or the Bearded Lake

21 Beddgelert, the Nanmor valley and the Pass of Aberglaslyn

Start:	Beddgelert
Distance:	8½ miles (13·5 km)
Approximate time:	5 hours
Parking:	Beddgelert
Refreshments:	Pubs and cafés at Beddgelert
Ordnance Survey maps:	Landranger 115 (Snowdon) and Outdoor Leisure 17 (Snowdonia – Snowdon area)

The dramatic Pass of Aberglaslyn

General description *This splendid walk in a majestic landscape provides outstanding views and scenic variety without any strenuous climbing or difficult terrain. From Beddgelert a pleasant and easy route, initially by the River Glaslyn and later along the shores of Llyn Dinas, is followed by a gradual ascent to near the head of the Nanmor valley. The route then descends equally gradually, much of it through delightful woodland, to Nantmor and continues to Pont Aberglaslyn before the highlight of the walk – through the beautiful and awe-inspiring Pass of Aberglaslyn back to Beddgelert.*

Refer to map overleaf.

Situated at a junction of roads, at the meeting of the Glaslyn and Colwyn rivers and surrounded by some of the highest mountains in Snowdonia, Beddgelert is an excellent walking centre with a variety of cafés, hotels, pubs and restaurants to cater for its many visitors. Some are drawn here as much by the legend of Gelert as its location. The story of the faithful dog Gelert, killed by its master Prince Llywelyn who wrongly thought that the dog had killed his baby son when in fact it had saved the child by killing a wolf, seems to have been a highly successful piece of publicity created by the landlord of the Royal Goat Inn in 1801. It was he who erected the cairn which is supposed to mark the dog's grave and which has since become a major tourist attraction. Near the meeting of the rivers is the attractive thirteenth-century church, on the site of an earlier Celtic monastery associated with St Celert, the latter more likely than the legendary hound to be the origin of the name of the village.

Start by the bridge and take the tarmac lane on its south side with the river on your left. Cross a footbridge by the confluence of the Glaslyn and Colwyn, bear slightly left, continue along the riverside path, and at a public footpath sign cross a lane and keep ahead, shortly climbing a ladder-stile. Continue along a most attractive rocky path between rhododendrons, which make a superb display in late spring, climb a ladder-stile beside a bridge and keep ahead along a narrow lane.

Pass through a metal gate and continue along a rough track to the entrance of the Sygun Copper Mine, where Victorian mine workings, abandoned in 1903, can be explored, with a full explanation of the processes of extraction and the life of the miners. Here turn left, following signs to Llyn Dinas, and bear right towards a bridge (**A**). Do not turn left over the bridge but follow footpath signs along a path, passing through a gate and continuing beside the river again. Climb a ladder-stile, and soon after passing a footbridge on the left you reach Llyn Dinas. Continue along the right-hand edge of the lake, go through a metal gate and keep ahead, climbing between rocks above the lake from which the views looking up Nantgwynant are superb. Descend to rejoin the lakeshore, passing to the left of a ruined house, and continue along the edge of woodland on the right for a few yards. After climbing a slight rise there is a small cairn on the right (**B**); here turn half-right over a low wall and take the path that heads uphill through the wood. The cairn and path are easy to miss – if you continue to near the end of the lake, you have gone too far and need to retrace your steps.

At first the path climbs steadily, then more steeply, to pass through a wall gap; here bear left and continue uphill to emerge from the woodland. Follow the path through an open, rocky landscape with grand mountain views

all around. At times it becomes indistinct but keep ahead, descending steeply, then climbing, dropping down slightly again and bearing right to pass through a wall gap. After a few yards bear slightly left to continue along an uphill and easily discernible rocky path, later descending to a ladder-stile. Climb it and bear right along a curving, grassy, uphill path through an area of rhododendrons, climb another ladder-stile and continue uphill through the dense bushes. Emerging from these you pass a house on the left; turn left around the end of it, go through a gate and keep ahead along a narrow path, heading gently downhill by a wall on the left. Continue past the end of the wall, later climbing gently to climb a ladder-stile by a small group of conifers on the right. Now keep by a wall on the right, descending steeply, turn right over a ladder-stile in the wall and then turn left, now with the wall on the left. Head downhill, then steeply uphill, pass through a wall gap and bear left, continuing to the top and passing through another wall gap. Now follow a path which bears right and heads downhill to a gate to the right of a house. Go through and keep ahead a few yards onto a narrow lane **(C)**.

Turn right to follow this lane through the Nanmor valley for ¾ mile (1·25 km), passing the remains of abandoned slate quarries. At a bridge turn right over a ladder-stile **(D)**, turn left over another one a few yards ahead and continue, bearing right away from the river and following a series of marker-posts. Cross a steam to enter woodland, rejoining the river to follow a delightful path which threads its way through trees and rocks.

Leave the woods to climb a ladder-stile and keep ahead, passing to the left of a house

SCALE 1:25 000 or 2½ INCHES to 1 MILE

some time. Pass to the left of the farmhouse, go through the right-hand one of a pair of metal gates ahead, cross the farmyard and go through another metal gate onto a tarmac drive (**E**). Turn left and follow this curving drive downhill, with superb views ahead of the Hebog range, passing through a metal gate and continuing as far as a house on the left. Here turn right (**F**) to pass through a wall gap, go down some steps and continue downhill across the field ahead, following marker-posts. Bear slightly right to the bottom end of the field, continue through a gap and on by a wall on the right to go through a gate. Head in a straight line across the next field, making for a marker-post and continuing to the left of a low, rocky outcrop to go through a metal gate. Continue along a track, passing houses, go through a kissing-gate and on down to a lane (**G**).

Turn right along this curving lane through the village of Nantmor, heading downhill to join a road. Turn right, shortly turning right again (**H**) into a car park; here turn left through a wooden gate, just before the toilet block, and immediately turn left again over a stone stile signposted Pont Aberglaslyn to enter National Trust property. Bear right along a stony, partially stepped path which heads uphill and curves left to a gate. Go through and continue through woodland, later keeping by a wire fence on the left, to descend to Pont Aberglaslyn (**J**).

There is a superb view from the bridge but do not cross it. Instead turn right along the riverside path through the Pass of Aberglaslyn. This is a most spectacular path – the river surges over rocks as it squeezes through the high, almost vertical walls of the wooded gorge – but it is quite difficult in places; it goes up and down and is rocky and narrow, and it is wise to look where you put every step. In a short while the hazards are left behind as you turn right up some stony steps soon after passing the entrance to a tunnel seen above on the right. Turn left to join the track of the disused Welsh Highland Railway. At first this railway carried visitors from near Caernarfon into the mountains and later it carried slate from local quarries down to the harbour at Porthmadog; it was closed in 1937. A short section has been reopened and there are plans to extend it.

Follow this flat, broad, easy track above the Glaslyn, passing through two short tunnels and turning left to cross the river (**K**). On the other side turn right to walk along a gentle, pleasant path across riverside meadows back to Beddgelert, passing through several gates. Just before reaching the village a short detour to the left leads to Gelert's grave. Finally pass to the right of the church, go through a metal gate and turn left to return to the starting point by the bridge.

and continuing gently uphill along the side of the valley. The path curves right and left to re-enter the woodland and keeps by a low wall on the left to a gate. Go through it and continue, climbing a ladder-stile and heading uphill to a marker-post. Keeping by a wall on the left, pass the left-hand side of a ruined house and continue over a stream. Where the path forks on the edge of woodland take the right-hand fork, initially heading uphill through trees and rocks but soon descending to pass through a wall gap. Continue, later joining and keeping by a wall on the right, and climb a stone stile in the wall where it bends to the left. Immediately turn right over a ladder-stile and turn left to go through a gate a few yards ahead.

Soon you join a track which bears right across a field and continues uphill into woodland. On emerging from the trees turn sharply to the left away from the track to go through a gap in a wall and head across the field to a metal gate in the far corner. Go through, continue along a grassy, partly slabbed path, with a wall on the right, passing through a wall gap and continuing across the next field towards the farm buildings ahead. At this point you may see some llamas – inquisitive but harmless creatures which have been in this area for

22 Betws-y-Coed, Gwydyr Forest and the Swallow Falls

Start:	Betwys-y-Coed, by the station
Distance:	8½ miles (13·5 km). Shorter version 5 miles (8 km)
Approximate time:	5 hours (3 hours for shorter version)
Parking:	Betws-y-Coed
Refreshments:	Pubs and cafés at Betws-y-Coed, Swallow Falls Hotel
Ordnance Survey maps:	Landranger 115 (Snowdon) and Outdoor Leisure 16 (Snowdonia – Conwy Valley area)

General description *This superb walk, lengthy but not strenuous, provides outstanding views, and passes through a great variety of scenery and terrain. An initial steady climb out of the Llugwy valley through the conifers of Gwydyr Forest leads to a fine viewpoint overlooking Llyn Elsi, and is followed by a descent along the line of a Roman road into the Llugwy gorge at the Miners' Bridge. The shorter version continues across the bridge to join the riverside path back to Betws-y-Coed but the full walk – definitely recommended unless short of time or energy – proceeds up through the beautifully wooded gorge to the Ugly House. Then the highlight of the walk is a magnificent 2½-mile (4 km) ramble beside or above the gushing, foaming waters of the Llugwy through both coniferous and deciduous woodland, passing the spectacular Swallow Falls and finally crossing delightful riverside meadows to Betws-y-Coed – undoubtedly one of the most attractive stretches of riverside walking in the country.*

With its dramatic location at the junction of three narrow, wooded, steep-sided valleys (Conwy, Llugwy and Lledr), it is easy to see why Betws-y-Coed became so popular with Victorian Romantics and artists and why it has developed into a major tourist and walking centre. The simple fourteenth-century church tucked away near the railway station possesses an effigy of Gruffydd ap Dafydd, nephew of Llywelyn, last native prince of Wales. In 1873 the church was superseded by a handsome Victorian Gothic

structure in the village centre. Some interesting and varied bridges span the rivers including the eighteenth-century stone Pont y-Pair (Bridge of the Cauldron), a suspension footbridge, and Telford's celebrated Waterloo Bridge, a cast-iron structure opened in 1815, the year of Wellington's famous victory, which carries the A5 over the River Conwy. For rainy days there is a comprehensive information centre, railway museum, motor museum and RSPB centre.

From the car park by the station cross an open, grassy area to the Victorian church and turn right along the main road. After just over ¼ mile (0·5 km) look out for some steps on the left, by a public footpath sign attached to a bus stop, which mark the start of the green waymarked Jubilee Path **(A)**. Go up these and take the steep, uphill, zigzag path through trees and bushes to reach a track. Turn left for a few yards and then turn sharp right along a narrow path through thick coniferous woodland. Although most of the

first part of this walk is through conifers, the route is fairly easy to follow because of the many green waymarks painted on rocks.

Continue uphill, bear slightly left to join a broad track, walk through a small clearing, and keep ahead where the track narrows to a path which plunges again into thick woodland. This delightful path, rocky, narrow and steep in places, curves upwards all the time and gaps in the trees reveal some grand views to the left over the Conwy Valley. Cross another track and continue uphill, passing through a gap in a wall, over a track and shortly afterwards bearing left at a T-junction. Bear slightly right on joining a broader path, cross a track and continue along the path ahead, eventually emerging from the trees to climb to a fine viewpoint overlooking Llyn Elsi.

Descend towards the lake and at the monument to Lord Ancaster – from which there are superb panoramic views that include Moel Siabod, the Glyders and Carneddau – turn sharp right (B) along a narrow path which heads downhill, keeping ahead to re-enter the trees and reach a drive. Cross straight over and take a narrow forest path, by a white walker waymark, which keeps along the edge of trees, by a wall on the right. Climb a ladder-stile, continue towards the cottage of Hafod-las in front, and just before the buildings turn left up to a ladder-stile beside a gate. Climb it and continue along a track which bears left uphill, soon meeting another broad, stony track. Here turn right, later bear right at a T-junction of tracks, and at the second track on the left go through a metal gate marked Pant-yr-hyddod. Continue along the track, now through open country, passing to the left of a house, go through a gate and continue up a steep, grassy slope which soon flattens out.

Keep ahead across a pleasant, open, grassy area – there is no obvious path – in a straight line, heading downhill towards the edge of conifers and a stile. Just before

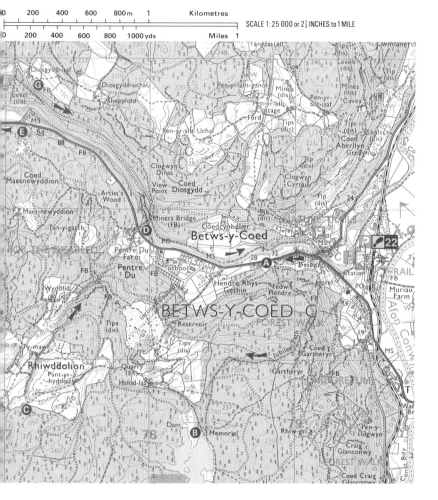

SCALE 1:25 000 or 2½ INCHES to 1 MILE

The Swallow Falls make an impressive sight

reaching the trees turn right downhill to join a clear track **(C)**. The ruined buildings ahead are of the deserted quarrying village of Rhiwddolion. Turn right along this blue-waymarked track, which is on the line of the Roman road of Sarn Helen, by a wall on the left and below a wooded embankment on the right. Head downhill for nearly 1 mile (1·5 km) along the right-hand edge of the Rhiwddolion valley, through several gates and over several tracks, following the blue waymarks all the time. Soon after crossing a footbridge climb a ladder-stile beside a gate, continue down to a metal gate, go through it and continue to the main road. Cross the road and take the path opposite, by a footpath sign.

Those wishing to do only the shorter version of the walk can descend the steps to the river, cross the Miners' Bridge and turn right to return to Betws-y-Coed.

Turn left, at an Artists Wood sign **(D)**, to follow a delightful, undulating path through the thickly wooded Llugwy gorge, between the road on the left and the rocky, surging river on the right. This yellow-waymarked path is part of the Artists Wood Walk, so named because of the many Victorian artists who were attracted to this area, in particular the Birmingham painter David Cox who painted many pictures around Betws-y-Coed. After ¾ mile (1·25 km) the path turns left, by a ruined building, up to the main road **(E)**.

Turn right and follow the road for 1 mile (1·5 km) (there is a path on the right-hand side all the way), going past the Swallow Falls Hotel and turning right over a bridge opposite Ty-hyll (the Ugly House). This gets its name from the rough, irregular blocks of stone used in its construction and was supposedly built in one day. It is now owned by the Snowdonia National Park Society and is open to the public.

At a public footpath sign turn right **(F)** down some steps to follow a riverside path across meadows. In a while turn left through a gap in a broken wall and continue beside the river, entering lovely woodland and soon passing above the spectacular Swallow Falls, which are particularly impressive after heavy rain. Stiles on the right over a wire fence enable closer views and better photographs.

Soon after passing the falls the path forks; here bear left, turning right to cross a footbridge over a stream and continuing to a house. Keep to the left of the house, go through a wooden gate, continue along a pleasant green path which soon re-enters coniferous woodland, cross another footbridge and keep ahead along a track which soon joins a tarmac lane **(G)**.

Follow this lane through the tall conifers — there are some particularly impressive Douglas firs on the right — high above the surging river. After ¾ mile (1·25 km), at a point where the lane bears gently to the left, turn right — there is no clear path — down through the woodland, soon following a wooden handrail on the right and heading steeply downhill to rejoin the river at the Miners' Bridge, a wooden bridge built at a steep, almost 45-degree tilt and once used by local miners to get to and from work. Do not cross it but turn left to follow a wooded riverside path. Soon after climbing a ladder-stile continue across meadows dotted with fine old trees, climb a stile and pass through more woodland to reach the stone arches of Pont-y-Pair. Turn right over the bridge and turn left along the road through Betws-y-Coed to return to the starting point.

23 The Roman Steps and Bwlch Drws-Ardudwy

Start:	Llyn Cwm Bychan — eastern end of lake
Distance:	8½ miles (13·5 km)
Approximate time:	6 hours
Parking:	Llyn Cwm Bychan
Refreshments:	None
Ordnance Survey maps:	Landranger 124 (Dolgellau) and Outdoor Leisure 18 (Snowdonia — Harlech & Bala areas)

General description The Rhinogs provide some of the most spectacularly rugged terrain in Snowdonia and this walk, which encircles the 2,363-foot (720 m) peak of Rhinog Fawr, enables appreciation of the stark beauty and sense of remoteness of this highly distinctive region without demanding any strenuous climbing. Starting from the shores of the delightful Llyn Cwm Bychan, the route makes use of two passes through the mountains that were formerly used as pack-horse trails and drove roads. The first of these is Bwlch Tyddiad, ascending via the well-known Roman Steps, and the second is Bwlch Drws-Ardudwy between Rhinog Fawr and Rhinog Fach. In between there is a short section through Coed y Brenin Forest. Although there is little actual climbing, in such rugged country the going is inevitably rough at times, especially in the latter stages of the walk across pathless, heathery moorland with a steep and quite difficult descent to Gloyw Lyn. In view of this the walk should not be attempted in bad weather, and those who want to enjoy the majestic scenery without the difficult sections near the end would be advised to walk as far as either the top of the Roman Steps, or the entrance to the forest, and then retrace their steps to Llyn Cwm Bychan.

Refer to map overleaf.

Llyn Cwm Bychan lies near the head of a beautiful valley at the end of a narrow, winding lane, surrounded by woodland and cradled by the rough, craggy landscape of the Rhinogs — a peaceful, remote and highly atmospheric spot. Start by walking to the far end of the car park, climb a ladder-stile and turn right along a path signposted 'Roman Steps'. This gently ascending path is well

waymarked; keep at first by a wall and later a wire fence on the right to reach a ladder-stile. Climb it and continue through lovely ancient oak woodland, now by a wall on the left, heading steadily uphill to climb another ladder-stile, here leaving the woods **(A)**. Head across an open, rocky and increasingly wild landscape, following a stream which is crossed several times, along a path which winds upwards to pass through a gap in a wall.

Now begins the ascent of the Roman Steps, heading up through the narrow defile of Bwlch Tyddiad below the steep slopes of Rhinog Fawr to the right. The steps are a most impressive piece of engineering but despite their name are more likely to have been constructed as part of a medieval pack-horse trail, though it is likely that this convenient route through the mountains was used even before the Romans came to this area. At the top of the pass and just before a cairn, bear slightly left and continue along a clear path that heads downhill, with extensive views ahead over mountain, moorland and the plantations of Coed y Brenin, briefly joining a wall on the right but then bearing slightly left away from it. Continue down between grass and heather to the edge of the forest, here climbing a ladder-stile and following a path through the dense conifers. Turn right to cross a footbridge over a stream and then follow the direction of a white walker waymark to the left to cross another footbridge and keep ahead — the path here is likely to be boggy. Coed y Brenin means the King's Forest, the royal person in question not a medieval Welsh prince but King George V; the forest was named in commemoration of his Silver Jubilee in 1935. It is an extensive area of mainly conifers, first planted by the Forestry Commission in 1922, and contains some small gold mines.

Soon after crossing another footbridge you reach a broad, forest track **(B)**. Turn right along it for ½ mile (0·75 km), continuing along the left-hand track at a fork and bending right to reach a T-junction. Turn right here and where the track bends sharply to the left **(C)** keep straight ahead along a grassy path which climbs gently to reach a gate on the edge of the forest. Go through to re-enter the Rhinog National Nature Reserve and continue across moorland, making for the gap between the twin Rhinog peaks. The path climbs gently to the head of the pass of Bwlch Drws-Ardudwy, passing through a wall gap, and it then descends equally gently, with spectacular views ahead, between rocks and heather, through the pass. Later the narrow pass broadens out into the gentler valley of Cwm Nantcol. Go through a metal gate and continue by a wall on the left which was joined earlier, passing through another metal gate to reach a footpath sign to the right of the farm of Maes-y-Garnedd **(D)**. This farm was the birthplace of John Jones, a brother-in-law of Oliver Cromwell and one of the judges who signed Charles I's death warrant in 1649. He was executed for this deed following Charles II's restoration in 1660.

At the footpath sign turn right along a track up to a metal gate on which a notice says 'Nantcol, Footpath Only, Private Road'. Go through the gate, follow the track ahead which winds gently uphill — at first between rocks and later between walls — to pass through a metal gate. Immediately turn left, at a footpath sign by a wall on the left, go through another metal gate and turn right along a grassy path, by a wall on the right, passing behind a house. Now bear left steeply uphill, looking out for a white marker-post by a tree. From here there are lovely views of the summit of Rhinog Fach. Continue uphill to another marker-post, go through a gap in a wall just beyond it and turn right, by a wall on the right, along a pleasant, grassy, gently ascending path. Where the wall bears right keep straight ahead to go through a metal gate, continue uphill and at the second white marker-post turn right **(E)** to follow a rather boggy path across rough grass. Go through a wall gap, continue ahead to join and keep by a wall on the left and head gently uphill, climbing a broken wall in front. Now turn half-left to continue across heather, rocks and bilberry, keeping roughly parallel to a wall on the left and making for a wall corner; here turn right along a narrow path, heading gently uphill to a small cairn.

Now for some rough, pathless walking. The cairn is as good a place as any to turn left off the path and head uphill in a northerly direction across the heather — there is a public footpath shown on the map around here but it seems to have disappeared — making for the top of the ridge ahead. The going is hard but there are no real difficulties and on reaching the ridge **(F)** there are magnificent all-round views — Gloyw Lyn and Cwm Bychan ahead, Rhinog Fawr to the right, Cwm Nantcol behind and the broad sweep of Cardigan Bay and the Lleyn Peninsula to the left. On the ridge a sheep fold acts as a landmark; pass to the right of it to pick up a discernible path which heads downhill towards Gloyw Lyn, keeping along the left side of the shallow valley and making for a ladder-stile. Climb it and then descend steeply to the lake — this is probably the most difficult part of the walk; there is no visible path down the rough, rocky terrain, so take care, and near the lake the ground becomes very boggy.

At the bottom bear left along what is now a clear path to keep by the left-hand side of this

remote, beautiful, small lake, continue around the far end and head back along the other side. After descending into a shallow gulley turn left **(G)** and head uphill between rocks. Continue along a path which now winds downhill between more rocks, heather and bilberry, bearing left, crossing a stream and heading down to a wall. Go through a gap in the wall and continue gently down towards the trees in front, crossing the accompanying stream several times.

Just before reaching the trees bear right to rejoin the outward route near the foot of the Roman Steps **(A)**. From here retrace your steps through the woodland to the starting point, enjoying the fine views to the left over Llyn Cwm Bychan on approaching the car park.

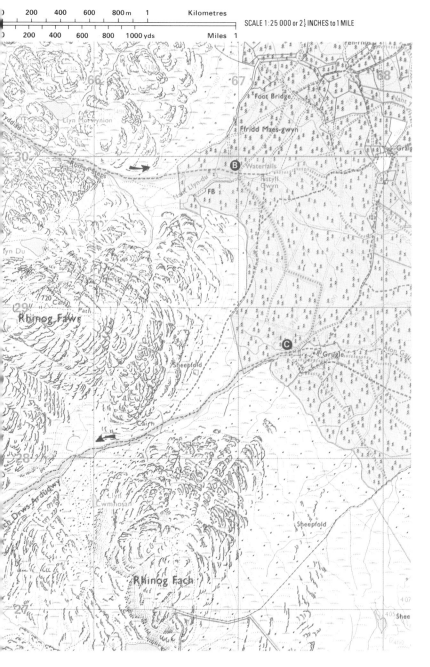

24 Cnicht

Start:	Croesor
Distance:	6½ miles (10·5 km)
Approximate time:	4½ hours
Parking:	National Park car park at Croesor
Refreshments:	None
Ordnance Survey maps:	Landranger 115 (Snowdon) and 124 (Dolgellau), Outdoor Leisure 17 (Snowdonia − Snowdon area) and 18 (Snowdonia − Harlech & Bala areas)

General description *Rising to 2,265 feet (690 m), Cnicht is possibly the most distinctive and easily recognisable of all the Snowdonia peaks, its prominent, pointed appearance when viewed from the south earning it the nickname the 'Welsh Matterhorn'. The ascent from Croesor is easier than it looks and is followed by a splendid scenic ridge walk to Llyn yr Adar before the route heads across to a disused slate quarry and gradually descends into Cwm Croesor for a relaxing final section. The route up Cnicht and along to Llyn yr Adar uses courtesy paths and walkers are urged to keep to the paths and comply with the Country Code. This is a walk best set aside for a fine day.*

Turn right out of the car park and walk through the village, passing a chapel on the right and continuing along the uphill tarmac track ahead. Descend to a ladder-stile, climb it and keep ahead along a rough track that heads up through woodland. On emerging into open country, about 100 yards (91 m) before reaching a ladder-stile ahead, bear right **(A)** at a white walker waymark along a broad, stony track which initially continues uphill but soon flattens out. From now on the distinctive, pointed shape of Cnicht is in sight most of the time.

Climb a ladder-stile beside a metal gate and continue through an increasingly wild and rocky landscape. The path, now grassy and narrower, heads gently uphill, bears right − at a white walker waymark − below a low, rocky cliff on the left and then bears left to descend to a ladder-stile. Climb it, bear left at another white walker waymark, heading directly towards Cnicht, and continue gently uphill more or less in a straight line. Shortly after meeting a wall topped by a wire fence on the right, turn right over a stile in the wall, then turn left to head downhill, keeping beside the wall and soon bearing right along

an obvious stony path below crags on the right.

Now the climbing is steeper, the path leading to a grassy plateau just below the final summit cone. Shortly after passing a cairn bear right for a short scramble, followed by a steep ascent along a path which zigzags between boulders to reach the summit **(B)**. From here there are majestic all-round views which take in the Cardigan Bay coast, the Hebogs, the Moelwyns and the Snowdon range in all its glory.

Continue by following an obvious path along the ridge, keeping to the left-hand side of the ridge as you descend, passing above the small Llyn Biswail on the left and eventually dropping down gently to Llyn yr Adar. To the left there is an outstanding view of Snowdon. The path keeps to the right of the lake, and just after passing some small rocky outcrops on the right reaches a cairn **(C)**. Turn right here along a path which is narrow and rather indistinct at times, heading downhill, with a superb view of the shapely profile of Moelwyn Mawr ahead; cross a stream and then continue uphill, the way indicated by a small cairn. Continue over the next ridge − again a small cairn shows the way − negotiating boulders and heading downhill to the small lake in front, Llyn Cwm-corsiog.

Walk along the right-hand side of the lake − this section is likely to be boggy − to the end of it where there is a small dam, and continue downhill below crags on the left, at first keeping parallel to a wire fence on the right but later bearing left and making straight towards the ruined quarry buildings ahead. There is a pleasantly melancholic air about the abandoned slate quarry. Pick your way through the mass of slates and in front of the main buildings turn right along the track of a disused railway **(D)**.

Just after a left-hand curve and just before the track reaches an embankment to curve right above the head of Cwm Croesor, look

out for a stony path on the left and turn off the track onto it. It is quite difficult to spot at first but it soon becomes a clear path which keeps below the crags on the right, descending and curving to the left. Then it broadens out into a stony track which keeps along the edge of Cwm Croesor below the steep and slaty slopes of Moelwyn Mawr. There are splendid views down the valley towards the Hebogs with Cnicht standing out prominently on the right. Much of this western face of Moelwyn Mawr is eaten into and disfigured by quarry workings and waste, but the deep caverns within it were put to good use during the Second World War as a hiding place for some of the nation's art treasures.

Go through a metal gate and continue, crossing an incline. To the right is a view of another incline at the head of Cwm Croesor.

The latter, the Rhosydd Incline, was opened in 1864 and linked the slate quarry with the end of the Croesor Tramway which carried slates from the local quarries to Porthmadog. It was worked by gravity, is 1,250 feet (381 m) long and rises 671 feet (205 m), with an average gradient of less than 1 in 2 although, as the information board at Croesor car park says, at the top the gradient is less than 1 in 1.

Now the track continues as a pleasant, grassy ledge, descending gently, later keeping by a wire fence on the right and crossing another incline. Turn right through a metal gate and head downhill towards farm buildings, curving left to join a farm track. Turn left along the track, go through a metal gate **(E)** and continue along the tarmac lane into Croesor, turning right at a junction to return to the car park.

SCALE 1:25 000 or 2½ INCHES to 1 MILE

25 Aran Fawddwy

Start:	Cwm Cywarch (at end of minor road 3 miles (4·75 km) north of Dinas Mawddwy)
Distance:	7½ miles (12 km)
Approximate time:	5½ hours
Parking:	Parking spaces at far end of common in Cwm Cywarch
Refreshments:	None
Ordnance Survey maps:	Landranger 124 (Dolgellau) and Outdoor Leisure 23 (Snowdonia — Cadair Idris area)

General description *It is popularly believed that the highest mountain south of the Snowdon range is Cadair Idris, but at 2,971 feet (905 m) Aran Fawddwy beats it by just 43 feet (13 m). While the former is the more interesting and dominating of the two, Aran Fawddwy is still a fine mountain to climb and looks most impressive, especially when viewed from the shores of Bala Lake. The route starts near the head of lovely Cwm Cywarch and climbs along the side of Cwm Hengwm, crossing the head of the cwm before heading for the summit. It is a lengthy and continuous, but steady rather than steep or strenuous, climb with some superb views;*

Looking towards Aran Fawddwy

the descent is rather featureless in its initial stages and has some tricky rocky sections. This walk is not recommended in bad weather and misty conditions, particularly in the winter, unless walkers are experienced in such conditions and able to use a compass.

Parts of the route use courtesy paths created by agreements between the landowners and the Snowdonia National Park Authority which are reviewed annually. Renewal depends on reasonable use and walkers keeping to the following conditions: keep to the footpath, do not camp, do not take dogs, use the stiles to cross fences and walls and leave no litter.

Start by walking along the narrow lane towards the head of Cwm Cywarch and turn right over a footbridge, at a public footpath sign and signs to Aran Fawddwy and Aran Benllyn **(A)**. Continue along a track, go through a metal gate and keep ahead along what is now an enclosed, winding path, following a public footpath sign around a sharp left-hand bend and heading uphill. The path joins a green track which continues up to a ladder-stile; climb it to follow a very pleasant track along the side of Cwm Hengwm. A few yards after crossing a

SCALE 1:25 000 or 2½ INCHES to 1 MILE

0 _____ 1 Kilometre

0 _____ ½ mile

stream bear right onto a narrow uphill path and keep along it, over several streams and ladder-stiles, climbing steadily to the head of the valley.

At the top, by a noticeboard and a white walker marker-post, turn left onto the start of the courtesy path (**B**). Follow a grassy path across a rather boggy area, keeping roughly parallel with a wire fence on the right, and at a meeting of wire fences turn left over a

ladder-stile. Continue along a splendid ridge path with an almost sheer drop to the left; there are grand views to the left looking down Cwm Hengwm, and even more superb views to the right looking across to the Aran ridge, the summit of Aran Fawddwy and the small lake of Creiglyn Dyfi, source of the River Dyfi, nestling below rocky slopes. The ridge narrows to Drws Bach, the 'little door' (to Aran Fawddwy), and just ahead is a

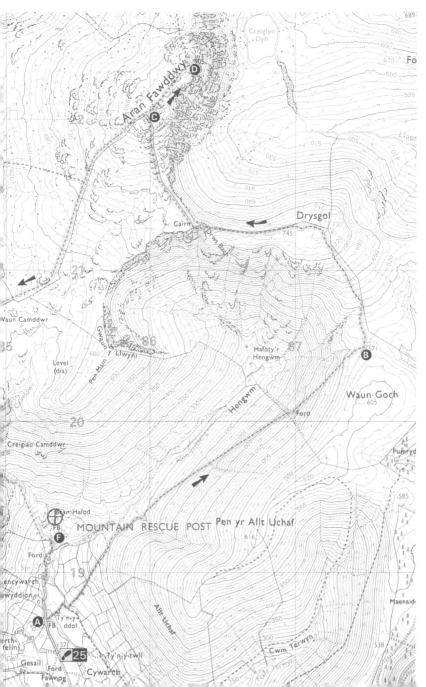

memorial cairn built to honour a member of an RAF mountain rescue team who was killed by lightning near here in 1960.

At this point follow the fence on the right as it bends to the right across an increasingly wild and rocky landscape. Ignore the first ladder-stile and continue by the fence, following it round to the left and up to another ladder-stile and meeting of fences (C). Climb the stile, keep ahead to a second ladder-stile but do not climb it; instead bear slightly right, at a footpath sign to Y Ddwy Aran, to keep by a fence on the left. Where the fence ends keep straight ahead in a north-easterly direction to reach the summit cairn of Aran Fawddwy (D), from where there are magnificent views which include Snowdon, the Mawddach estuary, Cadair Idris, the hills of mid Wales and Bala Lake.

Retrace your steps to the two ladder-stiles and meeting of fences (C) and turn right over the first stile. Turn left, following the direction of the footpath sign to Rhydymain, to head downhill, keeping by a fence on the left, across rather boggy, rocky and featureless moorland terrain. The path is not always clear, but keep by the fence all the way, following it around a right-hand turn down to a fence corner and ladder-stile.

Do not climb the stile but turn right and continue along to a pair of ladder-stiles. Turn left over the second of these and keep ahead, still by a fence on the left, to where the fence ends, continuing to join a path a little way ahead (E).

Turn left, cross a fence, continue to a footpath sign to Cwm Cywarch and a noticeboard by a small lake, and head downhill, by a fence on the right, into a dramatic, narrow and steep-sided cwm.

Cross a stream and follow it steeply downhill, along the side of a waterfall, through this wild, remote cwm, below sheer, overhanging crags on the right. As the rocky path descends the going becomes quite difficult in places and the rocks are likely to be slippery, but the route is marked by yellow arrows painted on them.

Descend to a footbridge and turn right over it, then turn left along the opposite side of the stream, now following an easier, clearer path which descends to a ladder-stile. Climb it, keep ahead for a few yards to a track and turn right along it (F), following it to the right and climbing two more ladder-stiles in quick succession. Continue along a path, by a wire fence and later a wall on the right, and on reaching a farm turn left towards a bridge. Do not cross it but turn right, at a yellow waymark, along a path that keeps by the right-hand side of a stream. Soon this joins a lane; follow it, still keeping by the stream, through a metal gate and back to the starting point.

26 Cadair Idris

Start:	National Park car park at Minffordd
Distance:	6 miles (9·5 km)
Approximate time:	5½ hours
Parking:	Minffordd car park
Refreshments:	None
Ordnance Survey maps:	Landranger 124 (Dolgellau) and Outdoor Leisure 23 (Snowdonia − Cadair Idris area)

General description *Cadair Idris means 'Chair of Idris', Idris being a shadowy, legendary figure − variously alleged to have been a giant, warrior king, astronomer and poet − who inhabited the mountain. Its shapely, distinctive profile, especially its long northern face, dominates the southern region of the National Park, making it a popular and interesting climb. This route ascends and descends by the well-known Minffordd Path, which involves a lot of climbing but rewards fit and energetic walkers with spectacular and varied terrain and extensive ever-changing views. Unless walkers are experienced in such conditions and able to use a compass, this is a walk to be avoided in bad weather, especially during the winter months, but one to be enjoyed to the full on a fine, clear day.*

At the far end of the car park turn left through a kissing-gate, by a public footpath sign, and turn right along a broad, tree-lined track. Cross a stream, bear left in front of a gate and continue along the track, by a wire fence on the right. Go through a kissing-gate, turn left to cross a stream and immediately turn right through a gate (the Idris Gate) (A) to enter the woodlands of the Cadair Idris National Nature Reserve.

The path winds steeply up steps through this beautiful ancient oak wood to a metal gate. Go through and continue, rather less steeply, into more open country, keeping above the tumbling stream on the right. Ahead are the steep rock and scree-covered slopes of Mynydd Moel and after a while the daunting, sombre cliffs of Craig Cau appear in front. Follow the cairned path as it bears left (B) and continues more steeply uphill onto a ridge to keep above Llyn Cau on the right. Llyn Cau is a perfect mountain cwm, its still, dark waters lying in a natural amphitheatre, enclosed on three sides by forbidding, almost sheer cliffs, and rising above it is Penygadair, the 2,928-foot (892 m) summit of Cadair Idris.

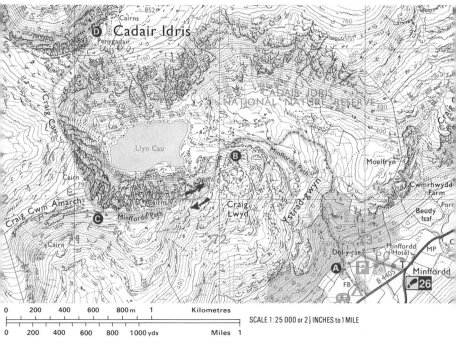

D Cadair Idris

Llyn Cau

CADAIR IDRIS
NATIONAL NATURE RESERVE

Craig Cwm Amarch

Minffordd Path

Craig Lwyd

Minffordd Path

Moelfryn

Cwmrhwydd Farm

Beudy Isaf

Minffordd Hotel

Dol-y-cae

Minffordd

26

```
0    200   400   600   800 m   1        Kilometres
0    200   400   600   800  1000 yds           Miles  1
```

SCALE 1:25 000 or 2½ INCHES to 1 MILE

Where the path flattens out for a while there are superb views to the left over the Tal-y-llyn valley, but soon the path bears right **(C)** and climbs steeply between rocks, heather and bilberry towards the top of Craig Cau. As you climb even more superb views open up to the left, over Tal-y-llyn Lake and along the valley looking towards Corris, backed by a glorious panorama of hills, moorlands and mountains. The path continues climbing steadily and curving to the right all the time along the rim above Llyn Cau, providing a series of dramatic views down the sheer cliffs to the lake far below from many different angles. This is the most scenic and exciting part of the walk, but it is a long, steep, rocky climb before reaching a ladder-stile at the top of Craig Cau.

Climb the ladder-stile and keep ahead across rocks to a prominent cairn before descending, still along the rim of the cliffs on the right, into Bwlch Cau, a col which lies between Craig Cau and Penygadair. Now comes the final assault on the summit. From Bwlch Cau follow a broad, cairned path which initially rises steeply, with lovely views to the left down the Dysynni valley to the coast, and continues less steeply and less clearly, although still marked with cairns, before a last steep but fairly short zigzag climb, scrambling over rocks and loose stones to the summit cairn, triangulation pillar and nearby shelter **(D)**. The extensive panoramic views are magnificent and include the Mawddach estuary, Cardigan Bay, the Lleyn Peninsula, the Snowdon range, the Rhinogs, Arenigs, Arans and the mountains of central Wales. The stone shelter replaced what used to be a refreshment hut provided for Victorian visitors.

There is no convenient circular route around Cadair Idris without involving long distances and quite a lot of road walking and therefore the best way to return to the start is to retrace your steps, enjoying more glorious views on the way down. Look out for the cairns in order to keep to the correct route and take great care; most accidents on mountains occur when people are descending and there are some awkward, eroded sections of loose stones to negotiate.

The distinctive outline of Cadair Idris

27 Snowdon

Start:	Pen-y-pass
Distance:	7½ miles (12 km)
Approximate time:	6 hours
Parking:	Pen-y-pass
Refreshments:	Café at Pen-y-pass, café at Snowdon summit station (restricted opening)
Ordnance Survey maps:	Landranger 115 (Snowdon) and Outdoor Leisure 17 (Snowdonia – Snowdon area)

General description *Sooner or later any serious walker in Snowdonia will want to tackle Yr Wyddfa – Snowdon itself – and, even though the 3,560-foot (1,085 m) summit may be shared with those who have come up the easy way on the mountain railway, it is a tremendously satisfying and exhilarating feeling to stand on the highest point in England and Wales surveying what is on a clear day a magnificent panoramic view. This route, which uses the Pig Track on the outward journey and the Miners' Track on the return, is one of the easier of several alternatives: the starting point is over 1,100 feet (335 m) up at the top of the Llanberis Pass and the paths are mostly well constructed and easy to follow. It must be emphasised, however, that this is a walk definitely to be avoided in bad weather and mist, especially during the winter or at any time when snow is covering the higher ground, unless walkers are equipped for and experienced in mountain walking in these conditions.*

With your back to the road, start by taking the path to the right of the car park. This is the Pig Track whose name has been a source of some controversy, but the likeliest derivation is that it leads to Bwlch y Moch, the Pass of the Pigs. It is a well maintained path which climbs steadily, using steps in places and giving fine views down the Llanberis Pass to Llyn Peris, bearing left to reach Bwlch y Moch **(A)**. Here the path to the steep, knife-edge ridge of Crib Goch leads off to the right – it is part of the classic Snowdon Horseshoe, one of the most challenging mountain walks in Britain – but you keep ahead along a flat, easy section of path, below the towering crags of Crib Goch and above Llyn Llydaw. There are superb views from here across the lake to the jagged cliffs of Y Lliwedd, another section of the Snowdon Horseshoe. Later the path passes

above the still, mysterious-looking waters of Glaslyn, which lies immediately below Snowdon itself whose distinctive, pyramid-shaped summit is now revealed.

After passing the Miners' Track which joins from the left **(B)**, the path starts to climb more steeply, bearing right and heading up a series of zigzags – this is the most strenuous part of the walk – eventually reaching the track of the Snowdon Mountain Railway by a tall marker stone **(C)**. The railway, a triumph of Victorian engineering in such terrain, is the only rack and pinion railway in Britain and was opened to passenger traffic in 1896. The journey from Llanberis to Snowdon's summit is about 5 miles (8 km) with an average gradient of 1 in 7. Although the purists decry the railway, especially the café and gift shop attached to its summit station, it does at least mean that hot drinks and something to eat are available, inducements used on many occasions to encourage reluctant walkers to make it to the top. Turn left and walk by the side of the track gently uphill for the short distance just over ¼ mile (0·5 km) to the station – the summit itself is just above it to the left **(D)**. The views from here, the highest point in Britain south of the Scottish Highlands, are magnificent; they extend over much of North Wales and in exceptionally clear conditions can include the Wicklow Mountains in Ireland, the Isle of Man and some of the higher Lake District peaks.

For the descent first retrace your steps to the junction of the Pig and Miners' tracks, taking care not to miss the tall stone **(C)** where you turn right away from the railway track. At the junction of the tracks **(B)** bear right onto the Miners' Track to head steeply downhill over rocks and scree to the shores

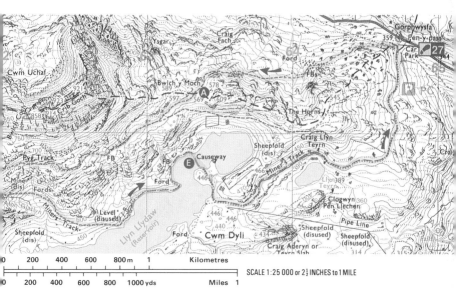

0	200	400	600	800 m	1	Kilometres
0	200	400	600	800	1000 yds	Miles 1

SCALE 1:25 000 or 2½ INCHES to 1 MILE

of Glaslyn – this is probably the most difficult section of the whole route, so be careful and take time. On reaching the lake follow the broad, fairly flat and well-constructed track along the shores of Glaslyn and later Llyn Llydaw, passing some of the ruined buildings of the Britannia Copper Mine. These include the miners' barracks and the large building beside Llyn Llydaw which was the ore-crushing mill. Near the end of the lake follow the track to the right across the causeway **(E)**, which was built in 1853 to make it easier to transport copper from the mines above Glaslyn to Pen-y-pass. It is obvious why the track is so broad, well-constructed and relatively flat. From the causeway there is a dramatic view of almost the whole of the Snowdon Horseshoe –

from the ridge of Crib Goch around to Y Wyddfa and along the cliffs of Y Lliwedd to Llyn Llydaw.

After crossing the causeway the track bears left and for a short distance keeps parallel with a pipe on the right which carries water from Llyn Llydaw to the nearby Cwm Dyli hydro-electric power station. The final section of the walk is most attractive. The track continues above the little Llyn Teyrn, where there are some more remains of miners' barracks, and from the track there is a final superb view behind of the summit of Snowdon. From here it leads back to Pen-y-pass with more spectacular views: to the right looking down Nantgwynant and ahead the impressive profiles of Moel Siabod and the Glyders.

Snowdon from the Miners' Track above Llyn Teyrn

28 The Glyders

Start:	Ogwen, at western end of Llyn Ogwen
Distance:	5 miles (8 km)
Approximate time:	6 hours
Parking:	Car park at Ogwen by youth hostel (if full, plenty of parking areas about ¼ mile (0·5 km) to east along A5)
Refreshments:	Light refreshments at Ogwen
Ordnance Survey maps:	Landranger 115 (Snowdon) and Outdoor Leisure 17 (Snowdonia − Snowdon area)

General description The Glyders lie between the Llanberis and Nant Ffrancon passes and overlook the Snowdon range to the west and the Carneddau to the east. They take their name from the twin peaks of Glyder Fach and Glyder Fawr, both of which are climbed on this walk. It is a magnificent, rugged and challenging walk amid superlative scenery − but it is also a strenuous walk suitable only for the fit and experienced mountain walker, as it involves some steep and energetic scrambling and difficult descents down scree and rock. It must be said too that this is definitely a walk for good summer weather, as even on a fine winter day snow and ice near the summits could make the going dangerous; it should only be tackled by walkers experienced in these conditions and properly equipped. But in the right conditions, when the views over the surrounding mountains are clear and extensive, this is a walk which will give tremendous exhilaration and satisfaction and will remain in the memory for a long while.

Start by taking the uphill, stony path at the side of the car park, by the refreshment kiosk and toilet block, climb a ladder-stile, cross a

SCALE 1:25 000 or 2½ INCHES to 1 MILE

The spiky pinnacles of Castell y Gwynt with Snowdon beyond, between the summits of Glyder Fach and Glyder Fawr

footbridge and continue; immediately there are excellent views of the Glyders in front and the distinctive bulk of Tryfan to the left. Where the main, well-constructed path bends to the right, keep ahead along a rather indistinct path making for Bochlwyd Falls in front. Climb fairly steeply to the right of the falls and at the top cross the stream on the left to continue along the left-hand side of Llyn Bochlwyd. Continue past the lake, climbing steadily to reach the col of Bwlch Tryfan and making for the ladder-stile ahead **(A)**.

From this col, which lies between Tryfan to the left and Glyder Fach to the right, there is a superb view looking back down to Llyn Bochlwyd and the whole length of the Nant Ffrancon Pass with the Menai Strait and Anglesey beyond. Climb the stile and turn right to begin the extremely steep and quite difficult ascent of Bristly Ridge, a daunting and formidable sight. There are two alternatives: either scramble up the rocks (if you like the challenge and have some experience — there are no exposed sections) or take the scree path to the left of the rock buttress. On reaching the top continue across the rocks to a prominent pile of boulders, which includes the well-known overhanging 'cantilever', and onto the weird-looking collection of rocks that constitute the summit of Glyder Fach at 3,262 feet (994 m) **(B)**. From here the views are breathtaking: a wide sweep takes in the Carneddau, Tryfan, Snowdon, the North Wales coast, Anglesey and Cardigan Bay, a superb panorama of the highest peaks south of the Scottish Highlands.

Continue to the next prominent group of rock pinnacles — Castell y Gwynt (the Castle of the Winds) — and either climb them or keep to the left of them. Descend and then climb again to rejoin the easy, gently ascending, cairned path to the summit of Glyder Fawr, with the impressive and familiar profile of Snowdon in the background all the while; the path keeps near the edge of the steep cliffs on the right to the summit, 3,279 feet (999 m) **(C)**, another widely scattered collection of rocks with magnificent views.

From here the descent begins and some care is required. Past the summit bear right to go down a steep, loose scree path to the small lake of Llyn y Cwn **(D)**. At the lake turn right across a boggy area to enter a broad shallow gully, after which there is a lengthy, rocky, steep climb down to Llyn Idwal, bearing left across the face of the cliff and descending by the right-hand side of the Devil's Kitchen. In Welsh this is appropriately called Twll Du (the Black Hole) as it is a dark, damp, deep, gloomy-looking cleft in the sheer rock face. In the latter stages of the descent a series of rocky steps helps the route down to the shores of Llyn Idwal.

The difficult and strenuous parts are over and now there is an easy, relaxing walk along the left-hand side of this beautiful lake, which is cradled by some of the most rugged and spectacular mountain terrain in Britain. Continue across the foot of the lake, cross a footbridge and turn left **(E)** through a metal gate to follow a broad, rocky path. Bear left to rejoin the outward route and retrace your steps to the car park at Ogwen.

If you have any energy left, it is worth turning left for a few yards to see the impressive Ogwen Falls, where the river flows out of Llyn Ogwen to descend into the Nant Ffrancon valley.

Useful organisations

The Countryside Commission
John Dower House, Crescent Place,
Cheltenham, Gloucestershire GL50 3RA.
Tel: 0242 521381

The Countryside Council for Wales
Plas Penrhos, Fford Penrhos, Bangor,
Gwynedd LL5 72LQ. Tel: 0248 370444

The National Trust
36 Queen Anne's Gate, London,
SW1H 9AS. Tel: 071 222 9251
(North Wales Regional Office, Trinity
Square, Llandudno, Gwynedd LL30 2DE.
Tel: 0492 860123)

Council for National Parks
246 Lavender Hill, London SW11 1LJ.
Tel: 071 924 4077

Snowdonia National Park Authority
National Park Office, Penrhyndeudraeth,
Gwynedd LL48 6LS. Tel: 0766 770274

National Park Information Centres can be
found at:
Aberdyfi (Tel: 0654 767321)
Bala (Tel: 0678 520367)
Betws-y-Coed (Tel: 0690 710665)
Blaenau Ffestiniog (Tel: 0766 830360)
Dolgellau (Tel: 0341 422888)
Harlech (Tel: 0766 780658)
Llanberis (Tel: 0286 870765)

North Wales Tourism Limited
77 Conway Road, Colwyn Bay, Clwyd
LL29 7LN. Tel: 0492 531731

Snowdonia National Park Society
Capel Curig, Gwynedd. Tel: 06904 287

The Ramblers' Association
1/5 Wandsworth Road, London SW8 2LJ.
Tel: 071 582 6878

The Forestry Commission
Information Branch, 231 Corstorphine
Road, Edinburgh EH12 7AT.
Tel: 031 334 0303

The Youth Hostels Association
Trevelyan House, 8 St Stephen's Hill,
St Albans, Hertfordshire AL1 2DY.
Tel: 0727 855215

The Long Distance Walkers' Association
7 Ford Drive, Yarnfield, Stone,
Staffordshire ST15 0RP.

The Council for the Protection of Rural
Wales
Ty Gwyn, 31 High Street, Welshpool,
Powys SY21 7JP. Tel: 0938 552525

Ordnance Survey
Romsey Road, Maybush, Southampton
SO9 4DH. Tel: 0703 792763/4/5 or
792792

Ordnance Survey maps of Snowdonia, Anglesey and the Lleyn Peninsula

The Snowdonia, Anglesey and Lleyn
Peninsula area is covered by Ordnance
Survey 1:50 000 scale (1¼ inches to 1 mile)
Landranger map sheets 114, 115, 116, 123,
124, 125, 135 and 136. These all-purpose
maps are packed with information to help
you explore the area. Viewpoints, picnic
sites, places of interest, caravan and camping
sites are shown, as well as public rights of
way information such as footpaths and
bridleways.

To examine this area in more detail, and
especially if you are planning walks,
Ordnance Survey Pathfinder maps at
1:25 000 (2½ inches to 1 mile) scale are ideal.

Maps covering the area are:

733 (SH 29/39/49)	771 (SH 86/96)
734 (SH 28/38)	785 (SH 45)
735 (SH 48/58)	786 (SH 65/75)
736 (SH 78/88)	801 (SH 34/44)
750 (SH 27/37)	821 (SH 13/23)
751 (SH 47/57)	822 (SH 33/43)
752 (SH 67)	825 (SH 92/93)
753 (SH 77/87)	843 (SH 12/22/32)
768 (SH 36/56)	885 (SH 70/SN 79)
769 (SH 56)	886 (SH 80/90)
770 (SH 66/76)	907 (SH 89/99)

Also at the same scale are the Outdoor
Leisure maps. Snowdonia – Conwy Valley
area number 16, Snowdonia – Snowdon
area number 17, Snowdonia – Harlech &
Bala areas number 18, and Snowdonia –
Cadair Idris area number 23 cover this area.

To get to Snowdonia use the Ordnance
Survey Routemaster map number 7 Wales
and the West Midlands at 1:250 000 (1 inch
to 4 miles) scale.

Ordnance Survey maps and guides are
available from most booksellers, stationers
and newsagents.

Index